Learn Spanish Like a Native *for Beginners* Collection

Learning Spanish in Your Car Has Never Been Easier! Have Fun with Crazy Vocabulary, Daily Used Phrases, Exercises & Correct Pronunciations

www.LearnLikeNatives.com

© Copyright 2021 By Learn Like A Native

ALL RIGHTS RESERVED

No part of this book may be reproduced, stored in a retrieval system, or transmitted in any form or by any means, without the prior written permission of the publisher.

CONTENTS

INTRODUCTION 2
CHAPTER 1 – THE FIRST IMPRESSION IS VERY IMPORTANT 11
CHAPTER 2 – ARE WE RELATED? 21
CHAPTER 3 – WHAT DAY IS IT? 30
CHAPTER 4 – THERE IS NO GIFT LIKE THE PRESENT. 44
CHAPTER 5 – HAVE A LOOK AROUND 58
CHAPTER 6 – HOW FAR CAN YOU COUNT? 70
CHAPTER 7 – WHAT DID YOU WANT TO BE WHEN YOU GROW? 78
CHAPTER 8 – WHERE ARE WE GOING? 90
CHAPTER 9 – SURVIVAL 101 98
CHAPTER 10 – WHAT IS THE COLOR OF THE SKY? 104
CHAPTER 11 – SO MUCH TO DO, SO MUCH TO SEE 110
CHAPTER 12 – I HAVE A LITTLE CRAVING 120
CONCLUSION 130
....133
CHAPTER 1 – DREAMING OF THE SOUTH 140
CHAPTER 2 – NOT ONLY BIRDS CAN FLY.....................160
CHAPTER 3 – LOOKING FOR A RIDE? 170
CHAPTER 4 – I FIND MY HAPPINESS WHERE THE SUN SHINES...182

CHAPTER 5 – I HAVE SO MANY STORIES TO TELL YOU 192
CHAPTER 6 – SO MANY ROADS AND SO MANY PLACES 217
CHAPTER 7 – EAT, TRAVEL, LOVE 227
CHAPTER 8 – SICK & ABROAD! 236
CHAPTER 9 – LEARN THE ROPES 244
CHAPTER 10 – BRING, LEARN & LEAD 254
CHAPTER 11 – NEW JOB, NEW LIFE 268
CHAPTER 12 – BRINGING HOME THE BACON 278
CONCLUSION 287
.... 289

Learn Spanish Like a Native *for Beginners - Level 1*

Learning Spanish in Your Car Has Never Been Easier! Have Fun with Crazy Vocabulary, Daily Used Phrases, Exercises & Correct Pronunciations

www.LearnLikeNatives.com

Introduction

Benefits of Learning Spanish

It is easy to stick with your native tongue. As an English speaker, you may feel as if you have a considerable advantage. But have you not ever been fascinated by other languages? By different cultures? Do you not find them captivating?

Let's say you are going to your holiday destination (maybe Spain, or even just a Spanish-speaking country). Did you think of everything? First aid kit, papers, and documents? Very good, but what about your foreign language skills? Have you ever thought about how you will express yourself? Unfortunately, many travelers neglect this topic and believe that with English, you can get anywhere. Some also assume you can communicate well with your hands and feet. The question you should ask yourself, though, is:

What do I expect from my journey, and which goals do I have (besides just relaxing, of course)?

To give you a little motivation, here are five advantages to being able to express yourself in the language of the country you are in:

- You get to know the locals much more authentically

- You understand the culture and attitude of people much better
- You can negotiate more effectively
- You do not waste valuable time, because you can communicate faster
- You feel safer

Just to keep it short, you do not have to learn a foreign language to perfection.

A Bit of History About This Beautiful Language...

We know Spanish as a poetic language. There's something about the way the string of words sounds like. It is as if it is meant to woo a lover.

This is why you may be surprised to discover that Spanish was actually derived from Vulgar Latin, the kind of Latin spoken by Roman soldiers. By 200 BC, this form of Latin became more popular and widespread throughout the Empire. Vulgar Latin gave birth to Spanish and other romantic languages we know today - Italian, French, Romanian, and Portuguese.

The Perfect Method

I'm sure you've been told there's no right or wrong way to learn a language. Well, that can't be right, because it's wrong! The truth is, most people don't lack in motivation, drive, excitement, determination, or even talent. More than anything, people lack the correct method.

I've been learning and teaching languages my whole life, and I've realized that the number one reason why people get stuck learning any language is simple. It's not because they are lazy, it's not because they don't have time, it's because they are bored!

You could go to the best schools and have the best teachers in the world, but if you're bored in your Spanish class, you're unlikely to get anywhere. Starting from scratch and ingesting new knowledge and can be a daunting thing as it is. So, if you're not fully engaged, learning a new language will be a long road.

Think about it. You've been a child before. Did you learn grammar before you knew how to speak? Of course not! So why do that now? In my opinion, that's where most language methods fail. Because they get caught up in all the specific rules and formal details a language holds, before worrying about whether or not their students understand what's going on. What's the point in knowing irregular verbs, if you can't even order food at the restaurant! My point being, unless you're planning to write a Ph.D. in Spanish, the most important thing for you is to be able to speak with other people.

That's where Learn Like A Native comes in!

With approximately 90 million people who speak and study Spanish as a non-native language, there's plenty of opinions as to what the best way to learn is.

That's why I based my method on modern expert research. The latest studies show that the most efficient way to learn languages – and Spanish in particular – is by learning vocabulary and grammar in conversation.

Using this method, I'll teach you how to apply formal knowledge in a real-life environment, through practical and relatable materials. With short and fun lessons, you'll stay engaged every step of the way, helping you retain vocabulary much more efficiently.

www.LearnLikeNatives.com

The audiobook version is narrated by a Spanish native speaker who will get you comfortable with the sounds of the language. You'll take an active part in the learning process and be required to speak, repeat, and exercise new sounds as they come up throughout the lessons.

Don't simply listen passively, but instead learn actively by practicing tough sounds such as the double "r," like a true native Spanish-speaker. If you have any trouble, the textbook will help you with written sounds so you can visualize letters and the sound they relate to.

You'll feel like you're in a Spanish class. But one you can take everywhere! With only 10 to 20 minutes per lesson, you can focus on each topic independently without any stress. Squeeze them into your schedule, sitting in your car or waiting for the Bus, and enjoy the flexibility of going through each step at your own pace. No one is watching you, of course, but I trust you'll do the work!

Learning a new language is a complex and rich experience. After you are done with this book, you will be ready (or more prepared) to travel, immerse yourself in Spanish-speaking cultures, read fiction and newspapers in Spanish, watch films, eat Latin American and Spanish foods, learn recipes, make Spanish-speaking friends, and, most importantly, enjoy yourself! This book is inspiring and vibrant to read and/or listen to, motivating you to speak and embrace the Spanish language, no matter how new, intermediate, or advanced you are to it.

Before you know it, you'll find yourself having a full-blown conversation in Spanish and wonder how you got there!

Are you ready? Okay, then we can start. Whichever language level you achieve depends entirely on you.

www.LearnLikeNatives.com

FREE BOOK!

Get the *FREE BOOK* that reveals the secrets path to learn any language fast, and without leaving your country.

Discover:

- The **language 5 golden rules** to master languages at will

- Proven **mind training techniques** to revolutionize your learning

- A complete step-by-step guide to **conquering any language**

www.LearnLikeNatives.com

www.LearnLikeNatives.com

www.LearnLikeNatives.com

Chapter 1 – The First Impression Is Very Important

Everyone knows the old saying, "You only get one chance to make a good first impression."

Therefore, it's no surprise that one of the first things every child learns is to say hello and introduce themselves. Even J.K. Rowling, the famous author of that young wizard's adventures, said "A good first impression can work wonders", and I completely agree.

Just a simple "Hello" can make all the difference in a conversation. That's exactly the reason why we will begin this exciting adventure with Spanish greetings. You will learn how to introduce yourself, greet people at different times of the day, and many other useful things.

We will start with the most popular greetings. There are several ways to greet people in Spanish, depending on who you are addressing and whether you want to be formal or not.

Ready to start? I really hope you are as excited as I am!

So, let's begin with the most common ways to greet someone in Spanish:

| Hello. | Hola. |

Oh-lah

Good morning.	Buenos días

Boo-eh-nos-dee-us

Just like in English, saying "Good morning" in Spanish is a compound expression, which also has different variables depending on the time of the day you are.

That way, you can find these other expressions.

Good afternoon.	Buenas tardes.

Boo-eh-nus-tar-des.

This is a good starting point for us. Tahr-des is a short but tricky word because that will help you perfect your pronunciation. You will have to "adjust" some of your consonants, starting with "t" and "r".

Spanish "t" sounds a lot like a British "t". It has a stronger sound, which concentrates on the tip of your tongue. Try it out loud: "t".

Now, the Spanish "r" is a bit more difficult. Especially because Hispanics have two sounds for it: one for a simple "r" and one for a double "r". Let us work for a second on the basics, and we will build it from there.

To make a Spanish "r", follow these instructions.

1. Lift your tongue inside your mouth, until the tip is somewhere between your incisive upper teeth and your hard palate.

2. Take a breath in and then breathe out –strongly- through your mouth. This should make your tongue move a bit, like a flapping. If it does not move, relocate your tongue until you find the spot.

3. Repeat again, until you master it.

4. Practice this until you are making a sound that is similar to a cat purring.

5. Once you have achieved this, start graduating the amount of air you use. This is important because the difference between a simple and double "r" depends on the amount of air you put into it.

How did it go for you? Do not worry if it doesn't work straight away. I couldn't do these sounds for a long time, but practice makes perfect and eventually, you too will be able to obtain beautiful and clear "r's".

Going back to our lesson, we have "Good night".

| Good night. | Buenas noches. |

Boo-eh-nus-noh-chess

As for a goodbye, "Buenas noches" is also valid, and recommended in the case of formal and more respectful gatherings. It is similar to the word "aloha". As you may know,

Hawaiians only use one word for both "hello" and "goodbye", which is "aloha". In a similar way, in Spanish, most greetings can also be used for both hello and goodbye.

You should also remember that, depending on whether you are greeting a friend or a stranger, you would use a different salutation.

For example, when entering a restaurant in the evening (or in any other formal occasion), you will say "Buenas noches" if you want to sound polite. Although, you can use "Hola" if you are meeting some old friends or greeting someone you already know (informal occasion).

How are you?	¿Cómo estás?

Koh-moh-s-tahs-too

You may have noticed that there is no literal translation, and the word "you" is not translated. While in English the pronoun is always used, in Spanish the ending of the verb usually makes it clear who the subject is, so no pronoun is necessary.

Asking "Cómo estás?" is a really good way to start a friendly conversation. It is an informal greeting and can also be used between people you are familiar with to ask about their health or mood.

How can I help you?	¿Cómo puedo ayudarte?

Koh-moh-poo-eh-doh-a-iu-dar-the

www.LearnLikeNatives.com

At this point, you have probably figured out the connection between two words: "how" and "cómo", and you know how important this word is in any language. This word is also important: "cuál".

| What is your name? | ¿Cuál es tu nombre? |

Koo-al-s-too-num-breh

An alternative to this phrase is "¿Cómo te llamas?", which is used just as often.

Koh-moh-te-ya-mus

To say what your name is in Spanish you use:

My name is	Mi nombre es
My name is John.	**Mi nombre es** John.

Me-num-breh-s

I am	Yo soy
I am new around here.	**Yo soy** nuevo por aquí.

Io-Soy

Thanks/Thank you.	Gracias.

Gra-cee-us

"Gracias" is used to say both "thanks" or "thank you". However, if you wish to show more gratitude, you could say "thanks to you", which translates to "Gracias a ti".

Gra-cee-us-ah-tee

I am sorry.	Lo siento.

Loh-see-n-toh

Nice to see you again.	Me alegra verte de nuevo.

Meh-ah-leh-gra-bur-teh-the-noo-eh-boh

Was it too hard? Don't worry. Greetings are basic phrases you will need to memorize, but I promise that the next sentences will be shorter and easier to remember.

What is new?	¿Qué hay de nuevo?

Ke-eye-the-noo-eh-boh

www.LearnLikeNatives.com

Another sentence with a similar meaning is "¿Qué me cuentas?" which directly translates to "What do you say?"

Ke-meh-ku-n-tus

| How are you doing? | ¿Cómo te va? |

Koh-moh-the-vah

| Goodbye. | Adiós. |
| **Goodbye**. I love you. | **Adiós**. Te amo. |

Ah-dee-os

This is a short way to say "bye". However, as already mentioned, if you want to be more formal, you can use "Good morning/afternoon/night", or "Hasta luego".

| See you later. | Hasta luego |
| Great! **See you later.** | ¡Genial! **Hasta luego.** |

Us-tah-loo-eh-goh

How are you sounding? Are you making sure to make a clear "t"? I hope so!

See you in a few.	Te veo más tarde.
Ok! **See you in a few.**	¡Okl! **Te veo más tarde.**

Ok-teh-be-oh-mus-tar-deh

As you might know, "Ok" is an English expression. Nevertheless, it's universally used worldwide, even among Spanish speakers. You should be aware, however, that there is a Spanish equivalent as well:

Ok.	Está bien.

Us-tah-bee-n

How is it going? Are you finding it difficult or is it easy? Maybe you need to practice a little bit more. Remember: practice is the key to mastery! Anyway, before we move to another topic, let's take a look at a short conversation that uses some of the words we have just learned.

Vendor   *Good morning!*

   Buenos días.

John: *Good morning to you, too.*

Buenos días para usted también.

Vendor: *How can I help you?*

¿Cómo puedo ayudarle?

John: *I am here to pick up a cake.*

Estoy aquí para buscar un pastel.

Vendor: *Sure. What is your name?*

Claro. ¿Cuál es tu nombre?

John: *My name is John Hill.*

Mi nombre es John Hill.

Vendor: *Oh, I am sorry. Your birthday cake is not ready yet.*

Oh, lo siento. Tu pastel de cumpleaños no está listo aún.

John: *Ok. When can I come pick it up?*

Está bien. ¿Cuándo puedo venir a recogerlo?

Vendor: *It will be ready in one hour.*

Estará listo en una hora.

John: *Great. I will run some errands and come back.*

Genial. Haré unas diligencias y regresaré.

Vendor: *Thanks for understanding. See you in a few.*

Gracias por entender. Te veo más tarde.

John: *Sure. See you later!*

Claro. ¡Hasta luego!

I hope John doesn't get low blood sugar, because he will have to wait for a while. In the meantime, shall we go and learn some new words and phrases that relate to family and relatives? This could be really handy if you were going to John's birthday party!

www.LearnLikeNatives.com

Chapter 2 – Are we related?

I am sure your family loves telling the story of your first word.

Language acquisition starts with receptive language, the understanding of sounds and words of the world around us. There is a good chance that either "mum" or "dad" (or a variable of these) was the first word you learned

Dad	Papá
My **dad** went out to get more ice.	Mi **papá** salió a conseguir más hielo.

Pah-páh

Accent marks are very important in the Spanish language. They can seem insignificant, but those tiny marks can completely change the meaning of a word. The accent on the à in "papà" - short on the first syllable and hard accent on the second, just as it happens with "mamá".

Mom	Mamá
My **mom** is there, by the corner.	Mi **mamá** está ahí, en la esquina.

Mah-máh

Son	Hijo
My **son** used to play tennis.	Mi **hijo** jugaba tenis.

E-ho

Daughter	Hija
My **daughter** likes to dance.	A mi **hija** le gusta bailar.

E-ha

In Spanish, there are two genders: every noun must be either masculine or feminine. hijo/hija is a good example. As a preliminary guide, it is good to know that singular:

- Nouns ending in "o" are masculine (male), with few exceptions;

- Nouns ending in "a" are nearly all feminine (female).

Throughout this book, we will see several examples of these. As a general rule, you can form the feminine or masculine version of nouns by changing the final vowel.

Therefore, you would use words like "hija" or "ellas" for females, and "hijo" or "ellos" for males.

Brother	Hermano
This is my **brother** Alex.	Este es mi **hermano** Alex.

Ehr-ma-no

Sister	Hermana
She is my **sister** Coreen.	Ella es mi **hermana** Coreen.

Ehr-ma-na

Uncle	Tío
I have two **uncles**.	Yo tengo dos **tíos.**

Tee-os

In the same way, as in English, in Spanish you form most plurals by simply adding an "s" to the end of every word. Just like you change from "uncle" to "uncles", you get a plural by turning "tío" into "tíos".

Aunt	Tía
My **aunt** has two kids.	Mi **tía** tiene dos hijos.

Tee-a

Cousin	Primo
My **cousin** lives far away from here.	Mi **primo** vive lejos de aquí.

Pree-mo

Grandfather	Abuelo
My **grandpa** picked up mangoes every day.	Mi **abuelo** recogía mangos todos los días.

Ah-boo-eh-loh

Grandmother	Abuela
My **grandma** loved knitting.	Mi **abuela** amaba tejer.

Ah-boo-eh-lah

How is it going so far? Don't you worry, we just need to meet a few more people, and then we can take a short break.

Siblings	Hermanos/Hermanas
I have three **siblings**.	Yo tengo tres **hermanos/hermanas**.

Ehr-ma-nos/ Ehr-ma-nas

Relatives	Parientes
I have many **relatives**.	Yo tengo muchos **parientes**.

Pah-ree-en-tes

This is a great word to practice your single "r". Remember that you create this the same way you do it for the double "r", but the amount of air that you breathe out is considerably lower, and it produces a softer sound.

Family	Familia
My **family** is big.	Mi **familia** es grande.

www.LearnLikeNatives.com

Fah-ee-lee-ah

Neighbor	Vecino
Dan is a great **neighbor**.	Dan es un gran **vecino**.

Beh-see-noh

How do you feel? Ready for a short practice? Great!

Allyson: *Happy birthday!*

¡Feliz cumpleaños!

Kelly: *Hello! Thanks a lot! I am happy that you came.*

¡Hola! ¡Muchas gracias! Estoy feliz de que hayas venido.

Allyson: *I am happy that you invited me.*

Yo estoy feliz de que me hayas invitado.

Kelly: *Sure. Let me show you who everyone is.*

Claro. Déjame mostrarte quién es todo el mundo.

Allyson: *Great!*

¡Genial!

Kelly: *That girl is my sister, and my cousin John is sitting next to her.*

Esa chica es mi hermana, y mi primo John está sentado junto a ella.

Allyson: *Yeah. Next to them is your brother Mark, right?*

Sí. Junto a ellos está tu hermano Mark, correcto?

Kelly: *Perfect! Yes. He picks me up from school sometimes.*

¡Perfecto! Sí. Él me recoge de la escuela algunas veces.

Allyson: *I remember.*

Lo recuerdo.

Kelly: *Good. By that other corner are grandma, grandpa and uncle Ed.*

Bien. En esa otra esquina están la abuela, el abuelo y el tío Ed.

Allyson: *Your grandma looks so young!*

¡Tu abuela luce tan joven!

Kelly: *Yes. I hope I have the same luck.*

Sí. Yo espero tener la misma suerte.

Allyson: *Don't we all?*

¿No lo deseamos todas?

Kelly: *Let's see... who's missing? Oh, well. Dad is outside, with the neighbors and the rest of the family.*

Veamos... ¿quién falta? Oh, bueno. Papá está afuera, con los vecinos y el resto de la familia.

Allyson: *Great! I can't wait to meet them.*

¡Genial! Yo no puedo esperar a conocerlos.

So, what do you think? Learning a new language is about listening to things over and over again and repeating many times. My advice is to always say the words out loud. This is an excellent way to practice a new language and, if you do so, you will see a significant improvement over the next chapters.

www.LearnLikeNatives.com

Chapter 3 – What day is it?

Learning how to measure and tell the time is hugely valuable. In many cultures, punctuality is extremely important and viewed as a form of respect, and I personally think it is a great sign of courtesy. Of course, learning the days of the week and months is also important, so you can make plans. Another thing you may want to know before leaving for a foreign country is what season is it, to know what to pack and dress accordingly.

As always, we will start with the basics:

Second	Segundo
One hour has sixty **seconds**.	Una hora tiene sesenta **segundos**.

Seh-goon-dos

Minute	Minuto
One hour has sixty **minutes**.	Una hora tiene sesenta **minutos**.

Mee-noo-tos

Hour	Hora
There are twenty-four **hours** in a day.	Hay veinticuatro **horas** en un día.

Oh-ras

An excellent moment to practice that single "r". Repeat with me: oh-ras. Good, let's continue.

Day	Día
January has thirty-one **days**.	Enero tiene treinta y un **días**.

Dee-us

Week	Semana
We have one **week** to finish.	Tenemos una **semana** para terminar.

Seh-mah-nah

Month	Mes

We will be there next **month**.	Nosotros estaremos allá el **mes** próximo.

Mess

Year	Año
It's the wedding of the **year**!	Es la boda del **año**!

Ah-nioh

Spanish has the "ñ" sound. Compared to an "n", this sound is very nasal.

To master the "ñ", you should start by pronouncing a "nioh" sound but really into the tip of your tongue. A perfect "ñ" sound resonates between your hard palate, the tip of your tongue and your nose. This is how you can start doing it.

1. Pronounce an "n" and maintain that sound. Feel how it resonates in the back of your mouth.

2. Now, try to take that sound "forward" by pushing it behind your upper teeth. Create a "nioh" sound if you need it. You will feel how it starts moving into the tip of your tongue.

3. Repeat as many times as you need.

Decade	Década
This **decade** is going to start soon.	Esta **década** va a empezar pronto.

The-ka-tha

Century	Siglo
This is the discovery of the **century**.	Este es el descubrimiento del **siglo**.

See-gloh

Morning	Mañana
The meeting was this **morning**.	La reunión fue esta **mañana**.

Mah-niah-nah

Afternoon	Tarde
Will you be there in the **afternoon**?	¿Tú estarás ahí en la **tarde**?

Tar-the

How is that double "r" sound going? Great! Let's keep moving.

Night	Noche
The moon comes out at **night**.	La luna sale en la **noche**.

Noh-che

Spring	Primavera
Everything flowers in **spring**.	Todo florece en **primavera**.

Pree-ma-veh-rah

Remember: that soft sound you need for "rah" will depend on the amount of air that you breathe out.

Summer	Verano
We had a fun **summer**.	Nosotros tuvimos un **verano** divertido.

Beh-rah-noh

Autumn	Otoño

| Look at the first **autumn** leaf. | Mira la primera hoja de **otoño**. |

Oh-to-nioh

| Winter | Winter |
| **Winter** has arrived. | Ha llegado el **invierno**. |

In-bee-er-noh

| January | Enero |
| **January** is the first month of the year. | **Enero** es el primer mes del año. |

Eh-ne-roh

| February | Febrero |
| That tree flowers in **February**. | Ese árbol florece en **Febrero**. |

Feh-breh-ro

| March | Marzo |

| **March** is a good month for harvesting. | **Marzo** es un buen mes para cosechar. |

Mar-soh

April	Abril
We stop activities in **April**.	Nosotros paramos las actividades en **Abril**.

Ah-breel

Have you noticed how most of the names of the months are similar between English and Spanish? That's a relief, right?

May	Mayo
May is going to be a great month.	**Mayo** será un gran mes.

Ma-ioh

June	Junio
The break starts in **June**.	El descanso comienza en **Junio**.

www.LearnLikeNatives.com

Hu-neo

July	Julio
July is a hot month in Spain.	**Julio** es un mes caliente en España.

Hu-lee-oh

August	Agosto
This **August** will be rainy.	Este **Agosto** será lluvioso.

Ah-gos-toh

September	Septiembre
Next semester starts in **September**.	El próximo semestre comienza en **Septiembre**.

Sep-tee-m-breh

October	Octubre
My birthday is in **October**.	Mi cumpleaños es en **Octubre**.

Ok-too-breh

November	Noviembre
We celebrated Halloween all **November**.	Nosotros celebramos Halloween todo **Noviembre**.

Noh-bee-m-breh

December	Diciembre
The year ends in **December**.	El año termina en **Diciembre**.

D-c-m-breh

Monday	Lunes
Today is **Monday**.	Hoy es **Lunes**.

Loo-ness

Tuesday	Martes
I have an appointment next **Tuesday**.	Tengo una cita el próximo **Martes**.

Mar-tess

Repeat again: mar-tess. This is a great word to practice the double "r" and the "t" sound. Remember that the Spanish "t" is very clear and strong, like the British one.

Wednesday	Miércoles
Wednesday is not a good day for me.	El **Miércoles** no es un buen día para mí.

Mee-er-ko-less

Thursday	Jueves
I'll see you next **Thursday**.	Yo te veré el próximo **Jueves**.

Hu-eh-ves

Friday	Viernes
The party is next **Friday**.	La fiesta es el próximo **Viernes**.

Bee-er-ness

Saturday	Sábado
I play every **Saturday**.	Yo juego cada **Sábado**.

Sah-bah-doh

Sunday	Domingo
We can have breakfast this **Sunday**.	Podemos desayunar este **Domingo**.

Do-meen-goh

How is it going? Are you ready for a short conversation?

Ally: So, what are your plans for the next year?

Así que, ¿cuáles son tus planes para el año que viene?

Juan: I honestly don't know what will happen after winter.

Yo honestamente no sé qué pasará luego del invierno.

Ally: *Will you at least come back in February? Spring is lovely here.*

¿Al menos vendrás en Febrero? La primavera es hermosa acá.

Juan: *If I don't, I promise I will be back to celebrate summer, in July.*

Si no lo hago, prometo que regresaré para celebrar verano, en Julio.

Ally: *Everyone loves summer. I love autumn.*

Todo el mundo ama el verano. Yo amo el otoño.

Juan: *Why?*

¿Por qué?

Ally: *Leaves change colors and I love the weather between September and November.*

Las hojas cambian de color y amo el clima entre Septiembre y Noviembre.

Juan: Two weeks ago you weren't loving it that much.

Hace dos semanas no lo estabas amando mucho.

Ally: Are you talking about that rainy Wednesday? I hated that.

¿Estás hablando de ese Miércoles lluvioso? Yo odié eso.

Juan: Yeah. As if it were not enough with those boring Mondays.

Sí. Como si no fuese suficiente con esos aburridos Lunes.

Ally: Oh, sure. I don't like Mondays. I love Fridays.

Oh, seguro. No me gustan los Lunes. Yo amo los Viernes.

Juan: Like everyone. But I like Saturdays better.

Como todo el mundo. Pero a mí me gustan más los Sábados.

Ally: Yes. Especially the ones in Spring, when you take your boat for a ride.

Sí. Especialmente los de Primavera, cuando sacas tu bote a dar un paseo.

Juan: You remember it. Good.

Tú lo recuerdas. Bien.

It's not as hard as you thought, right? There is a lot to remember, but sometimes it's easier if you find the similarities between English and Spanish, like as those in the names of the months. Again, practice makes perfect.

Now has come the time to learn some important verbs and how to conjugate them.

www.LearnLikeNatives.com

Chapter 4 – There is no gift like the Present

Just as in any other language, Spanish verbs are an important part of everyday speaking. When studying a foreign language, the present is the first tense you will learn, as this will allow you to form simple sentences. It is used to describe something that is happening right now or a state of being. Using the present tense, you will be able to speak about your desires, interests and plans.

First of all, in Spanish, verb conjugation is done by changing the ending of the verb. Verbs are divided into 3 different categories, called "conjugaciones" - conjugations. Each one is characterized by a specific ending in its infinitive form:

- First conjugation: Verbs ending in -AR (like amar)

- Second conjugation: Verbs ending in -ER (like creer)

- Third conjugation: Verbs ending in -IR (like vivir)

www.LearnLikeNatives.com

In this chapter I will teach you how to conjugate the regular verbs.

In addition, as you do in English, also in Spanish you can merge all the 3rd person singular pronouns. For your convenience, this is what we will do here.

Hopefully, with a bit of practice, you will realize that Spanish verb conjugation is actually much easier than it seems.

So, let's get started. There is no time like the present!

To love	Amar	Root	Termination
I love	Yo amo	Am-	Ar changes for "o"
You love	Tú amas		Ar changes for "as"
He/She/It loves	Él/Ella/Eso "ama"		Ar changes for "a"
We love	Nosotros amamos		Ar changes for "amos"

You love	Ustedes aman		Ar changes for "an"
They love	Ellos/Ellas aman		Ar changes for "an"

The root of all regular verbs never changes. As you can see, the root is the part preceding the infinitive ending. So, for example, in "Amar" the root is "Am-". Like we said, the root always remains the same, and different endings are added to denote the person, number or tense. Let's look at some examples.

I love the rain.	Yo amo la lluvia.
She loves the music.	Ella ama la música.
You love movies.	Ustedes aman las películas.
They love to play music.	Ellas aman tocar música.

Great! Here is a tip: using the above table you will be able to conjugate every other regular verb that ends in "-ar", all you have to do is add to the root the relevant ending, as we just did. Clearly, the same logic applies to verb of the second and third conjugation (-Er and -Ir). That's good to know, right?

Here are a few more examples. For the verb "to sing" - "cantar", you can separate the root "Cant-", and all you will need to do is to add the correct ending, as previously explained. The root of the verb "to eat" – "comer" is "com-", and for the verb "to share" - "compartir", the root is "compart-".

Think about what you like to do in your free time for a moment. What are your interests? What are you passionate about? Verbs are important to discuss all of these things.

To believe	Creer	Root	Termination
I believe	Yo creo		Er changes for "eo"
You believe	Tú crees	Cre-	Er changes for "es"
He/She/It believes	Él/Ella/Eso cree		Er changes for "e"

www.LearnLikeNatives.com

We believe	Nosotros creemos		Er changes for "emos"
You believe	Ustedes creen		Er changes for "en"
They believe	Ellos/Ellas creen		Er changes for "en"

You believe in loyalty.	Tú crees en la lealtad.
He believes in what he can touch.	Él cree en lo que puede tocar.
You all believe in yourselves.	Ustedes creen en ustedes mismos.
They believe in you.	Ellos creen en ustedes.

For verb "Creer" the root is "Cre-".

Following this rule, the actual change for the 1st person conjugation would be "Yo creeo". However, in Spanish we often employ contractions –as we tend to shorten many words. This way "Creeo" becomes "Creo". This is the only special case for this section.

So, what have you learned and what do you believe in? Repeat with me: "yo creo en….". Eventually, you will be able to better express yourself in Spanish, but –in the meantime- "yo creo en" is good enough.

Let's carry on with another important verb: "to live" – "Vivir". In this case, the root is "Viv-".

To nourish	**Vivir**	Root	Termination
I live	Yo vivo	Viv-	Ir changes for "o"
You live	Tú vives		Ir changes for "es"
He/She/It lives	Él/Ella/Eso vive		Ir changes for "e"
We live	Nosotros vivimos		Ir changes for "imos"

You live	Ustedes viven		Ir changes for "en"
They live	Ellos/Ellas viven		Ir changes for "en"

I live downtown.	Yo vivo en el centro.
She lives far away from here.	Ella vive lejos de aquí.
It lives on our rooftop.	Eso vive en nuestra azotea.
They live for singing and dancing.	Ellos viven cantando y bailando.

Now let's look at the present of the auxiliary verb "to be" – "ser". This verb is one of the most versatile, and you will use it a lot in Spanish: to introduce yourself, find out more about something or someone, describe places and things, etc. It is an auxiliary verb and its purpose is to help other verbs conjugate in compound tenses. In other words, it helps to create more complex sentences and tenses.

There is also another verb that can sometimes be used with the same meaning of "to be": "estar" – "to stay". While in English "to stay" is only used to describe your location, in Spanish it can also be used to describe a state of being.

That sounds complicated but let's break it down.

In Spanish, "verbo ser" applies in the following cases:

- When identifying or defining something. Like in "I am Latin-American" -"Yo soy Latino Americano"-, or in "I am Lucy" –"Yo soy Lucy".

- When describing something or someone's characteristics. As in "He is tall" – "Él es alto", or "They are smart" – "Ellos son listos".

- When locating the occurrence of an event, like "The meeting will be at my house" –"La reunión será en mi casa", or "The dinner is at five" –"La cena es a las cinco".

- When talking about the time of the day, weather, and such. As in "It is two at noon" –"Son las dos del mediodía", or in "It is summer" –"Es verano".

On the other side, we use "verbo estar" in these cases:

- When setting people and things in space. "I'm on the top of the world" –"Estoy en la cima del mundo"; "The shirt is on the bed" –"La camisa está sobre la cama".

- When talking of the state of something. "I am depressed" –"Estoy deprimido"; "She is pregnant" – "Ella está embarazada".

I know it may sound a bit confusing, but once you understand the differences, you will soon see how easy these are to use and how helpful they are to express yourself.

For the time being, let's see how to conjugate them.

To be	Ser	Estar
I am	Yo soy	Yo estoy
You are	Tú eres	Tú estás
He/She/It is	Él/Ella/Eso es	Él/Ella/Eso está
We are	Nosotros somos	Nosotros estamos
You are	Ustedes son	Ustedes están

| They are | Ellos/Ellas son | Ellos/Ellas están |

Here are some examples of the verb "essere".

I am a fanatic.	Yo soy un fanático.
She is a bit short.	Ella es un poco baja.
The party is around nine.	La fiesta es alrededor de las nueve.
It is two in the morning.	Son las dos de la mañana.

We have described someone and talked about the time.

Now, let's see some examples of the "verbo estar".

You are in the right place.	Tú estás en el lugar correcto.
She is worried.	Ella está preocupada.
We are alive.	Nosotros estamos vivos.

| They are on table 5. | Ellos están en la mesa 5. |

How does this sound? This will come with practice, so let's continue.

Alongside the verb "to be", the second most important verb in the Spanish language is "to have" – "Tener" –. It is an auxiliary and irregular verb that allows you to express numerous things: possessing something (literally or in a figurative way), communicate needs and desires, etc.

To have	**Tener**
I have	Yo tengo
You have	Tú tienes
He/She/It has	Él/Ella/Eso tiene
We have	Nosotros tenemos
You have	Ustedes tienen

| They have | Ellos/Ellas tienen |

I have a meeting.	Yo tengo una reunión.
It has big paws.	Eso tiene patas grandes.
We have a plan.	Nosotros tenemos un plan.
They have a place by the lake.	Ellos tienen un lugar junto al lago.

Are you looking forward to putting this into practice?

Emma: *Hi. I am Emma.*

Hola. Yo soy Emma.

David: *Nice to meet you. I am David.*

Encantado de conocerte. Yo soy David.

Emma: *Tell me, David. What do you like to do?*

Dime, David. ¿Qué te gusta hacer?

David: *I enjoy sailing on weekends.*

Yo disfruto navegar los fines de semana.

Emma: *Do you have a boat?*

¿Tú tienes un bote?

David: *Yes, I do. And what do you like to do?*

Sí, lo hago. ¿Y qué te gusta hacer?

Emma: *I have a dancing academy. I love to teach.*

Tengo una academia de baile. Yo amo enseñar.

David: *Really? I have a niece. She loves to dance.*

¿En serio? Yo tengo una sobrina. Ella ama bailar.

Emma: *Great! How old is she?*

¡Genial! ¿Cuántos años tiene?

David: *She is 6 years old. She turns 7 in two weeks.*

Ella tiene 6 años. Cumple 7 en dos semanas.

Emma: *I teach from the age of 7. Maybe you could bring her.*

Yo enseño a partir de los 7. Tal vez podrías traerla.

David: *Awesome. I am sure she will love it.*

Fabuloso. Estoy seguro de que le encantará.

As you can see, it is very important to know how to conjugate the Present simple. Just keep practicing until you achieve a better understanding.

Chapter 5 – Have a look around

Now, have a look around the room and tell me what you see. What's all around you? For instance, I usually keep a bottle of water on my desk and I always carry my mobile phone and wallet. In this chapter we will learn the names of a few things that you will probably have in your house.

Clock	Reloj
My **clock** says it is late.	Mi **reloj** dice que es tarde.

Reh-loh

Remember what we said at the beginning about punctuality? You will need a "reloj" to be always right on time.

Light	Luz
Turn the **light** on.	Enciende la **luz.**

Loose

Money	Dinero

www.LearnLikeNatives.com

| Spend your **money** wisely. | Gasta tu **dinero** sabiamente. |

Dee-neh-roh

| Bed | Cama |
| This **bed** is comfortable. | Esta **cama** es cómoda. |

Ka-mah

| Window | Ventana |
| That **window** points south. | Esa **ventana** apunta al sur. |

Venn-tah-nah

| Water | Agua |
| I want some **water**. | Quiero un poco de **agua**. |

A-goo-a

www.LearnLikeNatives.com

Car	Auto
That is a nice **car.**	Ese es un buen **auto**.

Au-to

Bicycle	Bicicleta
I took your **bicycle.**	Yo tomé tu **bicicleta**.

B-c-cleh-tah

Photo	Fotografía
I have your **photo** in my wallet.	Yo tengo tu **fotografía** en mi billetera.

Pho-to-gra-fee-a

News	Noticias
Did you read the **news**?	¿Tú leíste las **noticias**?

No-t-c-us

"Noticias" are very important to keep you informed. Let me give you a little advice. When preparing to visit another country, you should start reading local news sources from that place a couple of weeks before you get there. That will give you an insight into what is happening in the country and – why not – also some great talking points when you are speaking with locals.

Bin	Contenedor
I put it all in that **bin**.	Yo lo puse todo en ese **contenedor**.

Kon-teh-neh-door

Toothbrush	Cepillo de dientes
I need a new **toothbrush**.	Yo necesito un nuevo **cepillo de dientes**.

Seh-pee-io-deh-dee-n-ts

Mirror	Espejo

www.LearnLikeNatives.com

| That **mirror** looks dirty. | Ese **espejo** se ve sucio. |

S-peh-jo

| Laptop | Ordenador portátil |
| You can use my **laptop**. | Tú puedes utilizar mi **ordenador portátil**. |

Or-deh-nah-dor-por-tah-teel

| Computer | Computadora |
| That is my **computer**. | Esa es mi **computadora**. |

Kom-poo-tah-door-a

| Cellphone | Teléfono celular |
| I can't find my **cell phone**. | No encuentro mi **celular**. |

Ce-llu-lar

| Id | Identificación |

| Please, let me see your **ID**. | Por favor, déjame ver tu **identificación**. |

E-den-tee-fee-ka-sion

| Driving license | Licencia de conducir |
| You look funny in your **license**. | Tú te ves gracioso en tu **licencia de conducir**. |

Lee-cn-ce-a-the-kon-doo-cir

| Wallet | Billetera |
| Did you find your **wallet**? | ¿Encontraste tu **billetera**? |

Be-ye-teh-ra

Are you ready to create your own list? How many of those things are there in your house? Ok, let's use an example.

Nancy: *Honey! Do you have everything you need for camp?*

¡Cariño! ¿Tienes todo lo que necesitas para el campamento?

Peter: *Yes, mom. I think so.*

Sí, mama. Yo creo que sí.

Nancy: *Do you have your ID and phone?*

¿Tienes tu identificación y teléfono celular?

Peter: *Yes... I can't find my toothbrush.*

Sí. No puedo encontrar mi cepillo de dientes.

Nancy: *I saw it near the bathroom mirror.*

Lo vi cerca del espejo del baño.

Peter: *Thanks! Can I bring my laptop?*

¡Gracias! ¿Puedo llevar mi ordenador portátil?

Nancy: *To camp? No! Bring your wallet. You need that.*

¿Al campamento? ¡No! Lleva tu billetera. Necesitas eso.

Peter: *I need money, too.*

Necesito dinero, también.

Nancy: *It is on your bed.*

Está sobre tu cama.

Peter: *Good. I also need water and a small container.*

Bien. También necesito agua y un contenedor pequeño.

Nancy: *A container? Why?*

¿Un contenedor? ¿Por qué?

Peter: *For the food. Haven't you read the news? It's bear season.*

Para la comida. ¿Tú no has leído las noticias? Es temporada de osos.

Nancy: *Really? Ok. Keep your light close to you, just in case.*

¿De verdad? Ok. Mantén tu luz cerca de ti, por si acaso.

Peter: *Sure. Thanks, mom.*

www.LearnLikeNatives.com

Claro. Gracias, mamá.

I guarantee that if you follow the instructions and keep repeating our little lessons, you will make rapid progress and will soon be able to communicate fluently in Spanish. Feel free to go back to the previous chapters as many times as you like, all it takes sometimes is just a little something to jog your memory!

If you need help to count how many times you are repeating a sentence, move on to the next chapter: we are going to learn numbers next!

www.LearnLikeNatives.com

www.LearnLikeNatives.com

FREE BOOK!

Get the *FREE BOOK* that reveals the secrets path to learn any language fast, and without leaving your country.

Discover:

- The **language 5 golden rules** to master languages at will

- Proven **mind training techniques** to revolutionize your learning

- A complete step-by-step guide to **conquering any language**

www.LearnLikeNatives.com

Chapter 6 – How far can you count?

There are many nursery rhymes that help to introduce numbers even before a child understands numbers or how to count. It was probably through one of these songs that many of us learned numbers!

Don't worry. You won't have to do any math, just number learning!

When speaking in Spanish, you will often need to use and understand numbers to express time, record dates and – of course – count. So, here is a table to help you memorize them:

First, let's go with cardinal numbers. These numbers help us count objects.

		Pronunciation
One	Uno	Uh-noh

www.LearnLikeNatives.com

Two	Dos	Dos
Three	Tres	Tres
Four	Cuatro	Kua-troh
Five	Cinco	Sin-ko
Six	Seis	Seh-is
Seven	Siete	Si-eh-teh
Eight	Ocho	Oh-cho
Nine	Nueve	Noo-eh-beh
Ten	Diez	Dee-S
Eleven	Once	On-se
Twelve	Doce	Doh-se
Thirteen	Trece	Tre-se
Fourteen	Catorce	Ka-tor-se

| Fifteen | Quince | Kin-se |

As you can see, all the numbers from one to fifteen are specific words, and as such, you will have to learn it by heart. Let's see what happens from sixteen to nineteen.

Sixteen	Dieciséis	Dee-eh-si-seh-is
Seventeen	Diecisiete	Dee-eh-si-si-eh-te
Eighteen	Dieciocho	Dee-eh-si-oh-cho
Nineteen	Diecinueve	Dee-eh-si-noo-eh-be

Can you see that there is a pattern? You take the root, "dieci" and add the number that follows. "Dieci" is a word born from the contraction of two words: diez + y. So, basically, it translates as "ten and", as in "ten and eight" (dieciocho).

A similar thing happens to numbers from 21 to 29. We take the root number (veinte) and compress it. Doing this, we create a new root: "veinti".

Twenty	Veinte	Veh-in-teh
Twenty one	Veintiuno	Veh-in-tee-uh-noh
Twenty two	Veintidós	Veh-in-tee-dos
Twenty three	Veintitrés	Veh-in-tee-tres
Twenty four	Veinticuatro	Veh-in-tee-ku-ah-troh
Twenty five	Veinticinco	Veh-in-tee-sin-ko
Twenty six	Veintiséis	Veh-in-tee-seh-is
Twenty seven	Veintisiete	Veh-in-tee-si-eh-teh
Twenty eight	Veintiocho	Veh-in-tee-oh-cho
Twenty nine	Veintinueve	Veh-in-tee-noo-eh-be

Again, it is all about putting "veinti" and a number, together.

Don't worry. Things get way easier from now on.

| Thirty | Treinta | Treh-in-tah |

Thirty one	Treinta y uno	Tre-in-tah-e-uh-no
Thirty two	Treinta y dos	Tre-in-tah-e-dos

Starting on 30, numbers translate the same way they do for English. "Thirty + number" (30 + number). This way we get "treinta y cinco" (35), "cuarenta y cuatro" (44), "sesenta y yo" (60) or "ciento cuatro" (104).

Fourty	Cuarenta	Ku-ah-ren-tah
Fifty	Cincuenta	Sin-kuen-tah
Sixty	Sesenta	Seh-sen-tah
Seventy	Setenta	Seh-ten-tah
Eighty	Ochenta	Oh-chen-tah
Ninety	Noventa	No-ven-tah
One-hundred	Cien	Sien

| One thousand | Mil | Mill |

How is this going for you? Don't worry. This is one of those cases where you repeat and repeat, and in time you get it.

Let's move on to ordinal numbers. As the name suggests, they tell the "order" of things. That way, we can make ranks, prioritize, and set dates. Awesome, uh?

First	Primero	Pree-meh-roh
Second	Segundo	Seh-goon-doh
Third	Tercero	Ter-seh-roh
Fourth	Cuarto	Kuar-toh
Fifth	Quinto	Kin-toh
Sixth	Sexto	Sex-toh
Seventh	Séptimo	Sep-tee-moh
Eighth	Octavo	Ok-tah-boh

| Ninth | Noveno | Noh-beh-noh |

As is the case with cardinal numbers, each of the first ten ordinal numbers has a distinct form. Yet, you will see how easy this gets from now on.

Tenth	Décimo	The-see-moh
Eleventh	Décimo primero	The-see-moh-pree-meh-roh
Twelfth	Décimo segundo	The-see-moh-seh-goon-doh
Thirteenth	Décimo tercero	The-see-moh-ter-seh-roh
Fourteenth	Décimo cuarto	The-see-moh-kuar-toh
Fifteenth	Décimo quinto	The-see-moh-kin-toh

Starting on the 10th, there is a very easy formula. Just as we did with the cardinal numbers over 30, you split the number into two different parts and translate it. For example, 15th is the result of adding the 10th + the 5th. That way you get "Décimo quinto".

The 19th, therefore, is the combination of 10th and 9th. That way we get "Décimo noveno".

Easy right?

Chapter 7 – What did you want to be when you grow?

What did you want to be when you grew up?" How many times did someone ask you this question when you were a child? How many times have you changed your answer?

When I was little, I wanted to be a scientist. Later on, I wanted to be a singer. Nowadays I am a writer, but previously I have had different jobs. I have been a teacher, an electrician – honestly, not a very good one- and a chef.

We always need to remember that all professions are important. We need farmers to produce food of the highest quality, doctors to treat injuries and disease, artists to represent the beauty of the world around us, and bilingual writers to write Spanish for Beginners.

Speaking of artists, this is a good word to start with.

Artist	Artista
Picasso was an **artist.**	Picasso fue un **artista.**

R-tees-tah

www.LearnLikeNatives.com

You should always keep in mind that vowels like "a" are very open and clear in Spanish. "A" is pronounced like the English word "ah!". "Artista"

Chef	Cocinero
I want to become a **chef**.	Yo quiero convertirme en **cocinero**.

Ko-si-neh-ro

Construction worker	Obrero
My dad is a **construction worker**.	Mi papá es un **obrero**.

Oh-breh-roh

The Spanish "O" is also a very open vowel.

Firefighter	Bombero
Being a **firefighter** is a risky job.	Ser **bombero** es un trabajo peligroso.

Bom-beh-roh

Doctor	Doctor
The **doctor** will see you in 5 minutes.	La **doctora** lo atenderá en 5 minutos.

Doc-toh-rah

Unlike the English word "doctor", in the Spanish, the strong syllable is the second. Doc-tor.

Policeman	Policía
A **policeman** came to our house.	Un **policía** vino a nuestra casa.

Po-lee-c-ah

Teacher	Profesor
That is my **teacher**.	Esa es mi **profesora**.

Pro-phe-soh-rah

Let's put effort into this single "r". Proh-phe-soh-rah

Actor/Actress	Actor/Actriz

www.LearnLikeNatives.com

| Emma Stone is an **actress**. | Emma Stone es una **actriz**. |

Ac-trees

| Banker | Banquero |
| I am waiting for a **banker**. | Estoy esperando por un **banquero.** |

Ban-ke-roh

| Butcher | Carnicero |
| I am calling the **butcher** to order. | Estoy llamando al **carnicero** para ordenar. |

Kar-nee-se-roh

| Dentist | Dentista |
| I have a great **dentist**. | Tengo un gran **dentista**. |

Den-tees-tah

| Driver | Conductor |

My **driver** is very fast.	Mi **conductor** es muy rápido.

Kon-dook-tor

How's that buzzing in your palate?

Electrician	Electricista
You need to call the **electrician**.	Necesitas llamar al **electricista**.

Eh-lek-tree-cis-tah

Farmer	Granjero
My grandpa was a **farmer**.	Mi abuelo era **granjero**.

Gran-he-roh

Hairdresser	Estilista
I have a great **hairdresser**.	Yo tengo un gran **estilista**.

S-t-lis-tah

Journalist	Periodista
I will be a **journalist.**	Yo seré un **periodista**.

Pe-ree-oh-dees-tah

Lawyer	Abogado
My daughter is a **lawyer.**	Mi hija es **abogada**.

Ah-boh-ga-dah

Painter	Pintor
That **painter** did a good job.	Ese **pintor** hizo un buen trabajo.

Peen-tor

There are plenty of professions but don't worry, we won't go through them all. Just few more words.

Politician	Político
I want to be a **politician.**	Yo quiero ser un **político**.

Po-li-ti-coh

Psychologist	Psicólogo
I am a **psychologist**.	Yo soy **psicólogo**.

Si-ko-lo-go

Scientist	Científico
Scientists are addressing climate change.	Los **científicos** están abordando el cambio climático.

Sien-ti-fee-ko

What did you want to be when you grew up? Let's learn a few more words.

Plumber	Plomero
I have to call the **plumber**.	Tengo que llamar al **plomero**.

Ploh-meh-roh

Secretary	Secretario

My **secretary** is on vacation.	Mi **secretario** está de vacaciones.

Se-cre-ta-reeo

Shoemaker	Zapatero
The **shoemaker** did a good job.	El **zapatero** hizo un buen trabajo.

Sa-pah-teh-roh

Singer	Cantante
She's a great **singer**.	Ella es una gran **cantante**.

Kan-tan-teh

Waiter/Waitress	Mesonero/Mesonera
I'll call the **waiter**.	Llamaré al **mesonero**.

Me-soh-neh-roh

Writer	Escritor
It is hard to be a **writer**.	Es difícil ser una **escritora**.

S-kri-tor

Translator	Traductor
I work as a **translator**.	Yo trabajo como **traductora**.

Tra-duk-tor

Let's practice!

Cris: Hey! What do you have there?

¡Hola! ¿Qué tienes ahí?

Layla: It's a firefighter costume.

Es un disfraz de bombero.

Cris: Is it November yet?

¿Ya es Noviembre?

Layla: No! My son's school is going to have a "career day".

¡No! La escuela de mi hijo va a tener el "día de la carrera".

Cris: Oh, I see. I wanted to be a psychologist when I was nine.

Oh, ya veo. Yo quería ser psicóloga cuando tenía nueve.

Layla: I wanted to be a teacher. We are always changing, right?

Yo quería ser una profesora. Siempre estamos cambiando, ¿verdad?

Cris: Yeah. I wanted to be a teacher when I was fourteen.

Sí. Yo quería ser profesora cuando tenía catorce.

Layla: How did you decide to become a lawyer?

¿Cómo decidiste convertirte en abogada?

Cris: *Well... you know. I was seventeen and wanted to change the world.*

Bueno... tú sabes. Tenía diecisiete y quería cambiar el mundo.

Layla: *My son wants to be a farmer.*

Mi hijo quiere ser granjero.

Cris: *Isn't his dad a politician?*

¿No es su papá un político?

Layla: *Yeah. He started as a journalist and then changed careers.*

Sí. Él comenzó como periodista y luego cambió de carrera.

Cris: *Indeed. We are always changing.*

Efectivamente. Siempre estamos cambiando.

Now, repeat with me: "I wanted to be" -" Yo quería ser un" and complete the sentence.

One of the first questions people ask to someone they have just met is "What is your job?" which translates to "Che lavoro fai?". Thanks to what we have just learned in this unit, you are going to be ready for this conversation!

What next? Let's learn how to ask for directions.

Chapter 8 – Where are we going?

Being able to clearly tell where you want to go is very important, especially when traveling in another country. For this reason, the ability to communicate in simple situations such as asking for directions can make your life easier, in case of a SatNav failure or during a relaxing afternoon walk, when you don't have your mobile with you.

Street	Calle
That is the main **street**.	Esa es la **calle** principal.

Ka-ie

Avenue	Avenida
This is Libertador **Avenue**.	Esta es la **Avenida** Libertador.

A-ve-nee-da

Block	Cuadra

We are going to the **block** party.	Nosotros vamos a la fiesta de la **cuadra**.

Kua-drah

Square	Plaza
The **square** should be a few blocks ahead.	La **plaza** debería estar algunas cuadras más adelante.

Plah-sah

Are you pronouncing those vowels properly? Remember the open vowels!

Building	Edificio
This **building** has 110 floors.	Este **edificio** tiene 110 pisos.

E-dee-fee-sio

Monument	Monumento

| This **monument** is 300 years old. | Este **monumento** tiene 300 años. |

Mo-nu-men-to

| Hospital | Hospital |

| The **hospital** is 5 minutes away. | El **hospital** está a 5 minutos. |

Hos-pi-tal

Unlike the English "hospital", in Spanish, the strong syllable is "tal". The last syllable. In addition, make sure to make a clear "t". Hos-pi-tal.

| Corner | Esquina |

| The store is passing that **corner.** | La tienda está pasando esa **esquina**. |

Es-ki-nah

| Nearest | Más cercano |

| That is the **nearest** mall. | Ese es el centro comercial **más cercano**. |

Mas-ser-kah-no

| Turn left | Girar a la izquierda |
| You should **turn left** in two blocks. | Deberías **girar a la izquierda** en dos cuadras. |

Hi-rar-ah-lah-is-ki-er-dah

| Turn right | Girar a la derecha |
| Let's **turn right** after this corner. | Vamos a **girar a la derecha** luego de esta esquina. |

Hi-rar-ah-lah-deh-reh-chah

| Go straight on | Seguir recto |
| You only have to **go straight** on and you will get there. | Solo debes **seguir recto** y llegarás. |

Se-geer-rrek-toh

"Recto" has a strong double "r" sound in its first syllable, unlike "derecho", which is supposed to have only a soft "r" sound in its second one.

Go past	Pasar
You have to **go past** the main street.	Tienes que **pasar** la calle principal.

Pah-sar

Crossroads	Encrucijada
Take the left on the **crossroads.**	Toma la izquierda en la **encrucijada**.

N-kru-c-ha-dah

Those phrases will take you wherever you desire! Are you ready to put into practice what we have just learned about directions?

John: ¡Hey, sir! Good afternoon.

¡Hola, señor! Buenas tardes.

Vendor (Vendedor): What can I do for you?

¿Qué puedo hacer por ti?

John: Can you tell me how I can get to the train station?

¿Puedes decirme cómo llego a la estación de tren?

Vendor Sure. You have to go in that direction for three blocks.

Claro. Tienes que ir en esa dirección por tres cuadras.

John: I have to go past the library?

¿Tengo que pasar la biblioteca?

Vendor Yes. Then, you turn left and go for another five or six blocks.

	Sí. Luego doblas a la izquierda y sigues por cinco o seis cuadras.
John:	*Oh, I think I came from there. But I got confused at the crossroads.*
	Oh, creo que vengo de ahí. Pero me confundí en la encrucijada.
Vendor	*Happens all the time(Very usual). You have to go left at the crossroads.*
	Muy usual. Tienes que tomar la izquierda en la encrucijada.
John:	*Ok.*
	Está bien.
Vendor	*You will see a square. The station is in front.*
	Verás una plaza. La estación está al frente.
John:	*Thank you very much.*
	Muchísimas gracias.

www.LearnLikeNatives.com

Vendor: *No worries. Have a nice trip.*

No te preocupes. Que tengas un feliz viaje.

Are you ready to go and explore a new place? Better hurry! "Survival 101" is coming.

www.LearnLikeNatives.com

Chapter 9 – Survival 101

Each chapter contains helpful information, but this is particularly important. We have already said that: sometimes things go wrong. Your child may feel unwell, you could twist an ankle while hiking, lose your passport.... things do happen. So it's better to be prepared, right?

This sentence is pretty important:

Do you speak English?	¿Hablas español?

Ah-blas-es-pah-niol

This next one will make your life much easier.

Where is the bathroom?	¿Dónde está el baño?

Don-the-s-tah-el-ba-nio

How can I get to this place?	¿Cómo puedo llegar a este lugar?

Ko-moh-pooeh-doh-ie-gar-ah-es-the-loo-gar

| Where is the nearest hospital? | ¿Dónde está el hospital más cercano? |

Don-the-s-tah-el-hos-pee-tal-mas-ser-ka-no

Extremely important: "¿Dónde está el hospital más cercano?".

| When is the next flight? | ¿Cuándo es el próximo vuelo? |

Kuan-doh-es-el-proc-si-moh-vooe-lo

| Who can I talk to about this problem? | ¿Con quién puedo hablar sobre este problema? |

Kon-kien-pooe-doh-ah-blar-soh-bre-es-teh-pro-bleh-mah

| Where can I find a policeman? | ¿Dónde puedo encontrar a un policía? |

Don-the-pooe-do-en-kon-trar-ah-oon-poh-lee-c-a

Though I hope you will never need this:

| Where is the embassy? | ¿Dónde está la embajada? |

Don-the-s-tah-lah-m-bah-ha-da

| What do I need to visit...? | ¿Qué necesito para visitar...? |

Ke-neh-seh-si-toh-pah-rah-bee-ah-har

| Where can I find...? | ¿Dónde puedo encontrar...? |

Don-the-pooe-doh-en-kon-trar

Oh, I really hope you won't need some of them. But better safe than sorry! Let's see a short dialogue now.

Harry: *Hello, sir. How can I get to Kapital Burger, in Dos de Mayo Avenue?*

Hola, señor. ¿Cómo puedo llegar a Kapital Burger, en Avenida Dos de Mayo?

Driver: *I can take you, but is far. Is someone waiting for you? It's rush hour.*

Puedo llevarte, pero es lejos. ¿Alguien te está esperando? Es hora pico.

Harry: *No. I think I left my passport there.*

No. Creo que dejé mi pasaporte ahí.

Driver: It will take us at least 40 minutes to get there.

Nos tomará al menos 40 minutos llegar hasta allá.

Harry: Ok. Maybe I can talk to someone there.

Está bien. Tal vez puedo hablar con alguien ahí.

Vendor: Good afternoon. Kapital Burger.

Buenas tardes. Kapital Burger.

Harry: Hello! My name is Harry Klein. I was there last night, and I think I left my passport.

¡Hola! Mi nombre es Harry Klein. Estuve ahí anoche, y creo que dejé mi pasaporte.

Vendor: One second, please. Do you remember where were you sitting?

Un Segundo, por favor. ¿Usted recuerda dónde estaba sentado?

Harry: Yes. I was at the bar, by the corner.

Sí. Estaba en el bar, hacia la esquina.

Vendor: Ok. Give me a second.

Está bien. Dame un segundo.

Harry: Ok.

Está bien.

Vendor: Yeah. I just consulted my coworkers and they did not find anything. I am sorry.

Sí. Acabo de consultar a mis compañeros de trabajo y no consiguieron nada. Lo siento.

Harry: Thank you.

Gracias.

Driver: They didn't find it?

¿No lo encontraron?

Harry: No. Where is the nearest police station?

No. ¿Dónde está la estación de policía más cercana?

Driver: *Don't you want to go to your embassy? Could be better.*

¿No quieres ir a tu embajada? Podría ser mejor.

Harry: *Oh, yes. Where's the UK embassy?*

Oh, sí. ¿Dónde está la embajada del Reino Unido?

Driver: *Actually, it is near here. We will be there in a few minutes.*

De hecho, es cerca de aquí. Estaremos ahí en unos minutos.

What a nightmare to lose your passport abroad! I sincerely hope you will never have to use some of these phrases.

Now, let's move on to something less stressful. Shall we switch to colors?

Chapter 10 – What is the color of the sky?

I will tell you a secret: I love a wonderful view, and everywhere I go, I like to just lose myself gazing at the sky. I particularly love the sunset. I also like the sunrise, but I'm really not a morning person.

How many colors are there in the sky?

Yellow	Amarillo
My dress is **yellow**.	Mi vestido es **amarillo**.

Ah-mah-ree-io

Blue	Azul
The sky looks very **blue**.	El cielo luce muy **azul**.

Ah-sul

www.LearnLikeNatives.com

Red	Rojo
I bought a **red** car.	Yo compré un auto **rojo**.

Rro-ho

Purple	Púrpura
Those flowers are **purple**.	Esas flores son **púrpura**.

Poor-poo-rah

Pink	Rosa
My daughter wants a **pink** gown.	Mi hija quiere un atuendo **rosa**.

Roh-sah

Green	Verde
The fields look very **green** this year.	Los campos lucen bastante **verdes** este año.

Ber-des

Practice that "r" sound.

Orange	Naranja
I want my **orange** t-shirt.	Yo quiero mi camiseta **naranja**.

Nah-ran-ha

Brown	Marrón
Your dog is **brown**.	Tu perro es **marrón**.

Ma-run

Grey	Gris
Grey is a mixed color.	El **gris** es un color combinado.

Grease

Black	Negro
Black is my favorite color.	El **negro** es mi color favorito.

Neh-groh

www.LearnLikeNatives.com

White	Blanco
I painted the walls **white**.	Pinté las paredes de **blanco**.

Blan-ko

Fun fact: black and white are not colors. They represent, respectively, the absence of light and the lack of shadow.

No prizes for guessing what is coming now... Let's practice!

Lisa: *Hey, honey! I need your help with something.*

Hola, cariño. Necesito tu ayuda con algo.

Alex: *Yes, love. What is it?*

Sí, amor. ¿De qué se trata?

Lisa: *We need to pick the colors for the house before we move.*

Tenemos que escoger los colores para la casa antes de mudarnos.

Alex: *Oh, true. What do you have in mind?*

Oh, cierto. ¿Qué tienes en mente?

Lisa: *I was thinking of a light blue for our room, with touches of yellow.*

Estaba pensando en un azul claro para nuestro cuarto, con toques de amarillo.

Alex: *Ok. What have you thought of the living room?*

Está bien. ¿Qué has pensado para la sala?

Lisa: *I am thinking of a combination of red and white walls.*

Estoy pensando en una combinación de paredes rojas y blancas.

Alex: *Do you think that my black chair will match?*

¿Tú crees que mi silla negra combinará?

Lisa: *Absolutely(positive). And for the studio, I was looking for something more neutral.*

Positivo. Y para el estudio, estaba buscando algo más neutral.

Alex: *By neutral you mean...?*

¿Por neutral quieres decir...?

Lisa: *Earth colors. Like a light brown.*

Colores tierra. Como un marron claro.

Alex: *And the nursery?*

¿Y para el cuarto del bebé?

Lisa: *Grey, with a purple wall.*

Gris, con una pared púrpura.

Alex: *It sounds amazing. Thanks for planning all this.*

Suena asombroso. Gracias por planear todo esto.

Lisa: *Sure! I love it!*

¡Claro! ¡Me encanta!

What about you? Are you already planning to repaint your whole house? And for your dining room, would you like to go and buy some lanterns at an artisanal market in Mexico? Imagine all the things you could do! First of all, however, we need to get there. Let's go!

www.LearnLikeNatives.com

Chapter 11 – So much to do, so much to see

Where do you dream of going? Personally, I love the mountains. I grew up in a village in the valley, with stunning views of the mountains. I think maybe that's why I love mountains so much!

Now, imagine where you would like to go

Travel	Viaje
She lost the scarf during her last **trip**.	Ella perdió la bufanda durante su último **viaje**.

Bee-ah-he

Ticket	Boleto
I bought a two-way **ticket**.	Yo compré un **boleto** de ida y vuelta.

Boh-leh-toh

Airplane	Avión
This **airplane** is big.	Este **avión** es grande.

Ah-bee-on

Reservation	Reservación
He made a **reservation** for tonight.	Él hizo una **reservación** para esta noche.

Rre-ser-bah-sion

Re-ser-va-ción. Notice that accent in the last syllable.

Hotel	Hotel
I like this **hotel**.	A mí me gusta este **hotel**.

Ho-tel

Room	Habitación
They need a double **room**.	Ellos necesitan una **habitación** doble.

Ha-bee-ta-sion

www.LearnLikeNatives.com

Key	Llave
I lost my **key**.	Yo perdí mi **llave**.

Ya-beh

Passport	Pasaporte
Can I see your **passport**?	Puedo ver su **pasaporte**?

Pah-sah-por-te

Taxi	Taxi
Let's take a **taxi**.	Vamos a tomar un **taxi**.

Tac-si

"Taxi" is the same both in Italian and in English.

Car rental	Alquiler de autos
Where is the **car rental**?	¿Dónde está el **alquiler de autos?**

Al-ki-ler-the-au-tos

www.LearnLikeNatives.com

Bus	Autobús
We will take the **bus.**	Nosotros tomaremos el **autobús.**

Auto-bus

Subway	Subterráneo
The **subway** was out of service.	El **subterráneo** estaba fuera de servicio.

Sub-teh-rra-neo

Train	Tren
I'll take the **train.**	Yo tomaré el **tren.**

Tren

Let the "t" help you boosting the "r".

Station	Estación
That is the nearest **station.**	Esa es la **estación** más cercana.

Es-tah-sion

Theater	Teatro
This **theater** was remodeled 5 years ago.	Este **teatro** fue remodelado hace 5 años.

Teh-ah-tro

Beach	Playa
She wants to go to the **beach**.	Ella quiere ir a la **playa**.

Pla-ya

Mountain	Montaña
They want to climb that **mountain.**	Ellos quieren escalar esa **montaña.**

Mon-ta-niah

How is the "ñ" working for you' Have you been trying? Come on! Mon-ta-niah.

Island	Isla

www.LearnLikeNatives.com

Let's go to that **island**.	Vamos a esa **isla**.

Ees-lah

City	Ciudad
Mexico has big **cities**.	México tiene grandes **ciudades**.

Siu-dah-des

Are you ready? You know the drill. It's time to practice.

Shaun: *I want to buy the tickets for our trip. Can we decide on something?*

Quiero comprar los boletos para nuestro viaje. ¿Podemos decidir algo?

Vanessa: *Sure! Where do we want to go?*

¡Claro! ¿A dónde queremos ir?

Shaun: *Not another city. I want to rest.*

No a otra ciudad. Quiero descansar.

Vanessa: *I agree. Do you remember that beautiful mountain that Lisa showed us? Navarino Island.*

Estoy de acuerdo. ¿Tú recuerdas esa hermosa montaña que Lisa nos mostró? Isla Navarino.

Shaun: *Oh, sure. That cozy mountain house, right?*

Oh, por supuesto. Esa acogedora casa de montaña, ¿verdad?

Vanessa: *Yes. That one.*

Sí. Esa.

Shaun: *That sounds great. Do you think it is available?*

Eso suena genial. ¿Crees que esté disponible?

Vanessa: *On it!*

¡Estoy en eso!

Shaun: *Remember to check for a view.*

Recuerda buscar una vista.

Vanessa: *I got the perfect room! It is beautiful.*

Conseguí la habitación perfecta. Es hermosa.

Shaun: *Great. I need our passports to buy the tickets. I'll go get them.*

Genial. Necesito nuestros pasaportes para comprar los boletos. Iré a buscarlos.

Vanessa: *Sure. I am excited!*

Claro. ¡Estoy emocionada!

Repeat with me: "quiero viajar a" –I want to travel to-, then go out and make it happen! Traveling is an amazing way to meet new people and discover beautiful places. In my opinion, traveling is like growing up, except it never has to end.

A spontaneous trip, a last-second vacation… these are usually the best trips, the kind of stories you will remember forever.

And do you know what else I like when traveling? The food!

www.LearnLikeNatives.com

A Quick Message

A quick message before we start the final chapter of this book.

"No one can whistle a symphony. It takes a whole orchestra to play it." –

H.E. Luccock

Do you want to be part of the orchestra of the Learning Spanish community?

Here is how:

If you're enjoying this book, I would like to kindly ask you to leave a brief review on Amazon.

Reviews aren't easy to come by, but they have a profound impact in supporting my work. This way, I can keep creating new content to help the whole community at my very best.

I would be incredibly thankful if you could just take a minute to leave a quick review on Amazon, even if it's just a sentence or two!

www.LearnLikeNatives.com

It's that simple!

Thank you so much for taking the time to leave a short review on Amazon.

The community and I are very appreciative, as your review makes a difference.

Now, let's get back to learning Spanish!

www.LearnLikeNatives.com

Chapter 12 – I have a little craving

Food is a language itself. Food talks about soils, about culture, and about lifestyle. Whenever going to new places, having local food is fundamental for a trip that is complete.

However, we will let the locals introduce you to their exotic dishes. I will teach you some basics, though.

Potato	Papa
I want **potato** fries.	Yo quiero **papas** fritas.

Pah-pahs

Tomato	Tomate
You only need a few **tomatoes**.	Tú solo necesitas algunos **tomates.**

Toh-mah-tes

Corn	Maíz

Mexicans eat a lot of **corn**.	Los mexicanos comen bastante **maíz**.

Ma-ees

"Maíz" is fundamental. Mexicans discovered that corn is a very versatile ingredient.

Egg	Huevo
She wants **eggs** and ham.	Ella quiere **huevos** y jamón.

Ooe-boss

Cheese	Queso
I don't eat **cheese**.	Yo no como **queso**.

Ke-soh

Butter	Mantequilla
French people love **butter**.	Los franceses aman la **mantequilla**.

Man-te-ki-ya

"Man-te-qui-lla". Great for your taste buds.

Sandwich	Emparedado
We want five regular **sandwiches**.	Nosotros queremos cinco **emparedados** regulares.

Em-pa-reh-dah-dos

Burger	Hamburguesa
They want three **burgers**.	Ellos quieren tres **hamburguesas**.

Am-boor-ghe-sas

See?

Salad	Ensalada
I want a Caesar **salad.**	Yo quiero una **ensalada** César.

N-sa-lah-dah

www.LearnLikeNatives.com

Shrimp	Camarón
It has **shrimps** inside.	Eso tiene **camarones** adentro.

Ka-ma-roh-nes

Say again with me: ka-ma-roh-nes.

Sausage	Salchicha
We love **sausages** for breakfast.	Nosotros amamos las **salchichas** en el desayuno.

Sal-chee-chas

Bread	Pan
I bought the **bread** this morning.	Yo compré el **pan** esta mañana.

Pan

Chicken	Pollo
That **chicken** is raw.	Ese **pollo** está crudo.

Poh-io

Pancakes	Panqueques
These **pancakes** are fluffy.	Estos **panqueques** están esponjosos.

Pan-ke-kes

Rice	Arroz
The **rice** is ready.	El **arroz** está listo.

Ah-rros

If you want to eat rice, you better master that double "r". A-rroz.

Bacon	Tocino
The flavor of **bacon** is delicious.	El sabor del **tocino** es delicioso.

Toh-c-noh

Milk	Leche
I think this **milk** has gone bad.	Yo creo que esta **leche** se ha estropeado.

Leh-cheh

The "ch" sound in Spanish, is quite similiar to the English one. Our "ch" is the sound you would use to say "church", for example.

Cake	Pastel
You can eat more **cake**.	Tú puedes comer más **pastel**.

Pas-tel

Soup	Sopa
This **soup** is hot.	Esta **sopa** está caliente.

Soh-pah

Onion	Cebolla

I was chopping **onions**.	Yo estaba cortando **cebollas**.

Se-boh-yas

The Spanish sound for a double "l" is similar to the "y" in English, like in the word "yes".

Garlic	Ajo
You need to add **garlic** and stir.	Necesitas agregar **ajo** y remover.

Ah-ho

Lemon	Limón
These **lemons** look very nice.	Estos **limones** se ven muy bien.

Lee-moh-ness

Orange	Naranja
I want **orange** juice, please.	Yo quiero jugo de **naranja**, por favor.

Nah-ran-ha

Peanut	Maní
I am allergic to **peanuts**.	Soy alérgico al **maní**.

Mah-nee

"Maní" is an important one. It is, after all, one of the most common allergies around the world.

We are so close to finishing this first level!

Let's practice! Just one more!

Veronica: *I am hungry.*

        Estoy hambrienta.

Karol: *Let's see. There are still eggs, cheese and bread from the breakfast.*

        Veamos. Todavía hay huevos, queso y pan del desayuno.

Veronica: Uhm... Do we have potatoes and onions? It could use the eggs.

Uhm... ¿Tenemos papas y cebollas? Podría usar los huevos.

Karol: No. I couldn't go grocery shopping yesterday.

No. No pude ir de compras ayer.

Veronica: It's fine. Maybe I could go to that sandwich place, by the corner.

Está bien. Tal vez podría ir a ese lugar de emparedados, en la esquina.

Karol: I don't think it is open yet.

Yo no creo que esté abierto todavía.

Veronica: Oh... I could go for burgers, then. Do you want anything?

Oh... Podría ir por hamburguesas, entonces. ¿Quieres algo?

Karol: That sounds nice! Can you get me a salad?

¡Eso suena bien! ¿Podrías traerme una ensalada?

Veronica: *Sure! What kind of salad would you like?*

¡Seguro! ¿Qué tipo de ensalada te gustaría?

Karol: *Maybe a chicken Caesar salad.*

Tal vez una ensalada César con pollo.

Veronica: *Sounds good. I will come back soon.*

Suena bien. Volveré pronto.

How did this feel? I bet it was not that hard. I hope I am right because food is very important. Right?

Conclusion

Congratulations, you've made it! See, it wasn't too hard, was it?

As you realized by now, this wasn't your typical language book. If you tried and failed to learn Spanish in the past, you now discovered a new approach, one that you can build on to take your Spanish adventure to the next level. In going away from formal vocabulary and grammar lessons, together we shifted your focus from 'learning' Spanish to 'speaking' Spanish. Two very different things!

More than just the "rules" of Spanish grammar, today you have a sense of "the soul and music" of the Spanish language. You built a true solid foundation in Spanish and, even if you don't realize it yet, you are now capable of navigating social situations, create connections, keep contacts, as well as make friends. As I mentioned at the start, what's the point in knowing grammatical rules if you can't order your own food!

I won't bore you with the reasons why being able to speak another language is a huge benefit for you. Or why Spanish in particular will open a world of opportunities. I'm sure you're already convinced! But learning a new language is indeed a complex and rich experience, making this book a journey – your journey – into a new culture.

A beautiful culture you're now a part of.

No one is ever 'ready', so get out there! Travel, read fiction and newspapers in Spanish, watch films, eat Latin American and Spanish foods, make Spanish friends, and immerse yourself in Spanish-speaking cultures. Sure, you'll make a few mistakes at first. But who cares! You can always go back through our lessons and keep building your confidence. I'm sure you'll get there in no time.

This is just the first volume of this series, all packed full of vocabulary and dialogs, covering essential, everyday Spanish that will ensure you master the basics.

You can find the rest of the books in the series, as well as a whole host of other resources, at **LearnLikeNatives.com**. Simply add the book to your library to take the next step in your language learning journey. If you are ever in need of new ideas or direction, refer to our 'Speak Like a Native' eBook, available to you for free at **LearnLikeNatives.com**, which clearly outlines practical steps you can take to continue learning any language you choose.

A language should be lived, not just learned. So learn it, live it and, most importantly, enjoy it!

www.LearnLikeNatives.com

www.LearnLikeNatives.com

Learn Like a Native is a revolutionary **language education brand** that is taking the linguistic world by storm. Forget boring grammar books that never get you anywhere, Learn Like a Native teaches you languages in a fast and fun way that actually works!

As an international, multichannel, language learning platform, we provide **books, audio guides and eBooks** so that you can acquire the knowledge you need, swiftly and easily.

Our **subject-based learning**, structured around real-world scenarios, builds your conversational muscle and ensures you learn the content most relevant to your requirements.
Discover our tools at *LearnLikeNatives.com*

When it comes to learning languages, we've got you covered!

www.LearnLikeNatives.com

www.LearnLikeNatives.com

www.LearnLikeNatives.com

FREE BOOK!

Get the *FREE BOOK* that reveals the secrets path to learn any language fast, and without leaving your country.

Discover:

- The **language 5 golden rules** to master languages at will

- Proven **mind training techniques** to revolutionize your learning

- A complete step-by-step guide to **conquering any language**

www.LearnLikeNatives.com

www.LearnLikeNatives.com

www.LearnLikeNatives.com

Learn Spanish Like a Native *for Beginners - Level 2*

Learning Spanish in Your Car Has Never Been Easier! Have Fun with Crazy Vocabulary, Daily Used Phrases, Exercises & Correct Pronunciations

www.LearnLikeNatives.com

Chapter 1 – Dreaming of the South

You are sitting at home, thinking about vacation, and suddenly a friend calls you to tell you about their latest family travel to exotic South America--it was a beautiful, sunny, diverse, and entertaining place. You hang up and start imagining yourself with a Cuban mojito in hand, the sea in front of you.

Can you imagine kayaking with your family through the great blue sea of the Caribbean? Can you feel the hand of your loved one, the touch, while enjoying a glass of wine by the sunset? Just stay with me, because you can have it all.

To make this a reality, the first thing you need to search for are requirements, hotels, and transportation.

English	Spanish
To travel	Viajar

I want **to travel** to Cartagena.	Quiero **viajar** a Cartagena.

Vee-ah-har

Notice the "j" sound. For the Spanish language, "j" works the same way "h" does in English whenever preceding a vowel. For example, the word "house".

Now repeat: vee-ah-har.

Requirements	Requerimientos
Requirements to travel to Colombia.	**Requerimientos** para viajar a Colombia.

This is a typical "difficult" word for English speakers because Spanish has a different "r" sound. It has two different sounds: one for the "single r," and one for the "double r". We will not be too strict about this because it is mostly about practice. In any case, this is what I would recommend for pronunciation:

1. Lift your tongue and touch your hard palate with it. This is the space situated just behind your incisive upper teeth.

2. Breathe in and out through your mouth. This should make your tongue move at least a bit.

3. Repeat.

4. You can practice this until your "r" sounds like a kitten purring. Once you have achieved this, you can be confident you are getting it.

Back to requirements--checking this is very important: due to political and health challenges in many countries, it is possible that you may need some extra requirements to visit, such as vaccines or a travel visa.

Visa	Visa
Do I need a **visa** to travel to Colombia?	¿Necesito una **visa** para viajar a Colombia?

Please notice how the word "visa" is the same in both languages, as well as its pronunciation.

Next phrase.

Vaccines	Vacunas
Vaccines are needed to visit Colombia.	**Vacunas** necesarias para visitar Colombia.

"Vaccines" translates as "vacunas". This word can be split into three syllables: va-coo-nahs.

In case you have these requirements covered, the next step would be to look for flights.

Most airline platforms are multilingual. However, it is known that some domestic flights could be cheaper when bought with a national airline.

Airlines	Aerolíneas

What **airlines** travel to Cartagena?	¿Qué **aerolíneas** viajan a Cartagena?

This is a long and possibly difficult word, specifically because you need to use that single "r" sound. The sound difference between a single and a double will be given by the amount of air you breathe out. So, let's practice.

Ah-eh-ro-lí-neas

Something to keep in mind is that vowels in Spanish are very open and clear. For example, a Spanish "e" always has a similar sound as the one you would use to say "essay". That starting "e" sound is what we are looking for.

Flights	Vuelos
Find **flights** from Bogota to Cartagena.	Encontrar **vuelos** desde Bogotá hacia Cartagena.

You can notice how the word "from" translates to "desde", which is your starting point. While your destination is covered by "hacia".

One-way trip	Viaje de ida
Do you want a **one-way trip**?	¿Quieres un **viaje de ida**?

Round trip	Viaje de ida y vuelta
No, I want a **round trip**.	No. Quiero un **viaje de ida y vuelta**.

Dates	Fechas

Dates for your travel?	¿**Fechas** en las que viaja?

Repeat after me: Feh-chas

When looking for accommodations, you have many great references at your disposal, but it is always preferable to ask the locals for specifics related to the best and most touristy locations.

To stay	Alojarse
Best places **to stay** in Cartagena.	Mejores zonas para **alojarse** en Cartagena.

Touristic	Turísticas
Most **touristic** places in Cartagena.	Zonas más **turísticas** de Cartagena.

Once you have found somewhere you like, the next step is to book a room.

To Book	Reservar
I want to **book** a room.	Quiero **reservar** una habitación.

As you can see, this is another word where you need to put your double "r" into training. Repeat after me: reh-ser-var.

Good! Are we acing those r's or what?

Depending on how many people you include in your trip, you could choose a single room or a double room.

Single room	Habitación simple
I want a **single room.**	Quiero una **habitación simple**.

Double room	Habitación doble
I want a **double room**.	Quiero una **habitación doble**.

If you do not enjoy flying, perhaps other transportation methods could be useful.

Cruise	Crucero
I want a **cruise** through the Caribbean.	Quiero un **crucero** por el Caribe.

Crew-ce-ro

How do you feel so far? Ready to book a trip?

Great! Because now we are going to do some packing.

First, the verb that makes it happen: to pack.

To pack	Empacar
I need to **pack** my baggage.	Necesito **empacar** mi equipaje.

This is a double: you have "packing" and "baggage". These translate respectively as "empacar" and "equipaje".

With this in mind, repeat again: Necesito empacar mi equipaje.

Of course, you need a suitcase.

Suitcase	Maleta
I need a bigger **suitcase**.	Necesito una **maleta** más grande.

The word "maleta" can be used in general. However, similar to English, Spanish distinguishes a difference between your checked bags and your carry-on.

Checked bag	Maleta registrada
Your ticket includes one **checked bag**.	Tu boleto incluye una **maleta registrada**.

Carry-on	Equipaje de mano
Your **carry-on** is too big.	Tu **equipaje de mano** es muy grande.

With your suitcase on top of your bed, because that is how most of us do it, you are ready to start putting items inside.

Shirt	Camisa

I like this **shirt** for the trip.	Me gusta esta **camisa** para el viaje.

T-shirt	Camiseta
Why don't you bring a **t-shirt**? Something more sporty.	¿Por qué no empacas una **camiseta**? Algo más deportivo.

Pants	Pantalones
Should I bring some **pants**?	¿Debería llevar **pantalones**?

Shorts	Pantalones cortos
Maybe I should pack some **shorts**.	Tal vez debería empacar unos **pantalones cortos**.

Due to globalization, "shorts" is a common way to call short pants, even in Spanish speaking countries. Just in case, you have the neutral Spanish way.

Skirt/Dress	Falda/Vestido
I think I will pack a **skirt** and maybe a **dress**.	Creo que empacaré una **falda** y tal vez un **vestido**.

Skirt: fal-dah

Dress: ves-tee-doh

Sweater	Abrigo

I will bring a **sweater**.	Voy a empacar un **abrigo**.

This is a very useful one, so repeat: a-bree-goh. This is a word that can be used for "coat", from a sweater to a raincoat, and even shelter. Keep it in mind: "abrigo" will keep you warm if needed.

Underwear	Ropa interior
Pack **underwear** for a week.	Empaca **ropa interior** para una semana.

Socks	Calcetines
How many **socks** should I bring?	¿Cuántos **calcetines** debería llevar?

And, because we are already on it, it is a good idea to go through some body parts.

Feet	Pies
You have very cold **feet**.	Tienes los **pies** muy fríos.

Legs	Piernas
I have to shave my **legs**.	Tengo que rasurarme las **piernas.**

Hands	Manos
Do not forget the **hand** cream.	No olvides la crema de **manos.**

www.LearnLikeNatives.com

Arms	Brazos
I want to tan my **arms**.	Quiero broncearme los **brazos**.

Head	Cabeza
I got a bump on my **head**.	Tengo un chichón en la **cabeza**.

Face	Rostro
I need a **face** towel.	Necesito una toalla de **rostro**.

How are you doing so far? Are there any words you need to repeat?

After this short walkthrough of your body parts, I think we are ready to practice our first lesson. Shall we?

For this situation, we have prepared a call between you and a travel agent.

Agent: *Good afternoon! Where do you want to travel?*

¡Buenas tardes! ¿A dónde le gustaría viajar?

Allen: *Cartagena, Colombia.*

Cartagena, Colombia.

Agent: *Date for your travel?*

¿Fecha en la que viaja?

Allen: *December, 15th.*

15 de Diciembre.

Agent: *How many adults are traveling?*

¿Cuántos adultos viajan?

Allen: Two, please.

Dos, por favor.

Agent: Are you traveling with kids?

¿Viaja con niños?

Allen: Yes. Two kids.

Sí. Dos niños.

Agent: Would you like a one-way trip or a round trip?

¿Desea un viaje de ida, o un viaje de ida y vuelta?

Allen: Round trip. Thank you.

Viaje de ida y vuelta. Gracias.

Agent: When do you wish to come back?

¿Cuál fecha le gustaría para su regreso?

Allen: January, 2nd.

2 de enero.

Agent: Okay. Our lowest fare is $350 per person, but it does not include checked bags. Would you like to add checked bags?

Muy bien. Nuestra tarifa más baja es de $350 por persona, pero no incluye equipaje registrado. ¿Le gustaría añadir maletas registradas?

Allen: Not at the moment. Thank you.

No por el momento. Gracias.

Agent: Very well. Would you like to book accommodations?

Muy bien. ¿Le gustaría reservar alojamiento?

Allen: Sure. What do you have?

¡Claro! ¿Qué me ofreces?

Agent: I can offer you two bedrooms. One double with a King size bed, and another double with two single beds.

Puedo ofrecerle dos habitaciones. Una doble con una cama King, y otra habitación doble con dos camas individuales.

Allen: *Great!*

¡Genial!

Agent: *Perfect. Please, wait in line for a second so I can write down your details.*

Perfecto. Por favor, espere en línea para anotar sus datos.

How was this for you? Are you feeling more confident now? I hope you do, because we are about to take a flight.

www.LearnLikeNatives.com

Chapter 2 – Not Only Birds Can Fly

In my experience, airports can be stressful places for multiple reasons. They are crowded spaces with many lines to wait in and documents to show, and you have to do it every single time. Thankfully, I am here to help you be at your gate in time, stress-free.

Let's start by checking you in to your flight.

Passport	Pasaporte
Can I please have your **passport?**	¿Puedo ver su **pasaporte**?

Pah-sah-por-teh

Being by the counter, it is a perfect time to practice what we learned in lesson one. They will ask you where you are traveling, how many people are traveling in your family group, and the number of bags you have. Overweight luggage is a VERY common topic of discussion.

Overweight	Sobrepeso
This piece of luggage is **overweight**.	Esta pieza de equipaje tiene **sobrepeso**.

Come again: so-bre-pe-so

If you skipped the overweight experience—which I hope, because those fees are usually very high—you are ready to go through TSA.

Tray	Bandeja
Please take off shoes, coats, and metal objects, and put your belongings in a **tray**.	Por favor, retirar zapatos, abrigos y objetos de metal, y colocar sus pertenencias en una **bandeja**.

Remember what we learned in lesson one about the Spanish "j"? Time to practice that "ha" sound.

Ban-deh-ha

Screen	Revisión
Please, go to the left for a second **screen**.	Por favor, diríjase a la izquierda para una segunda **revisión**.

Re-vee-seeon

Once you are in, it is time to look for your gate.

Gate	Puerta
Where is **gate** 15?	¿Dónde está la **puerta** 15?

Poo-air-tah

Flight	Vuelo

What **flight** are you taking?	¿Cuál **vuelo** vas a tomar?

Voo-eh-loh.

Boarding pass	Pase de abordar
Please, have your **boarding pass** and passport in hand.	Por favor, tenga su **pase de abordar** y pasaporte a la mano.

This is a tricky one because it is a compound word. So, let's take it slow.

Pah-se-the-ah-bor-thar

Seat	Asiento
My **seat** is 23F.	Mi **asiento** es el 23F.

Ah-see-N-toh

Bathroom	Baño
Is that **bathroom** occupied?	¿El **baño** está ocupado?

Bah-nio

Blanket	Cobija
Can I have a **blanket**?	¿Me puede dar una **cobija**?

Koh-bee-ha

You know. I could teach you how to ask for other stuff… like some wine? Which is vee-noh (repeat with me: vee-noh), but let's be responsible and learn some emergency signals.

Go through	Pasar
I need to **go through**.	Necesito **pasar**.

Pah-sar

Feeling sick	Sentirse enfermo
I am feeling **sick**.	Me siento **enfermo**.

N-fur-moh

"Sick" translates directly as "enfermo". So, work on your phrasing, but especially remember that word, "N-fur-moh". Hearing "sick" in any language is a sign for help.

Headache	Dolor de cabeza
I have a **headache**.	Tengo **dolor de cabeza**.

Doh-lorh-the-ka-beh-sa.

Fever	Fiebre
I have a **fever**.	Tengo **fiebre**.

Fee-e-bre

www.LearnLikeNatives.com

Nausea	Náusea
I feel **nauseous.**	Siento **náuseas.**

Nah-ooh-ce-us

Allergic	Alérgico
I am **allergic** to...	Soy **alérgico** a...

Ah-ler-hee-koh

Needless to say, I hope you will not need any of this emergency speech, but we are here to be prepared for whatever comes our way.

How are you feeling so far? Think of the things we have just learned. You can now go into an airport, get into a plane, enjoy a movie, and land safely. Join me for a little practice.

Flight Attendant: *Hello! Boarding pass, please.*

¡Hola! Pase de abordar, por favor.

Cris:	*Hello!*
	¡Hola!
Flight Attendant:	*Welcome! You're at seat 14F. By the window.*
	¡Bienvenida! Su asiento es el 14F. Junto a la ventana.
Cris:	*Thanks!*
	¡Gracias!
Flight Attendant:	*What would you like to drink today?*
	¿Qué le gustaría tomar hoy?
Cris:	*I would like some water with ice.*
	Quisiera un poco de agua con hielo.
Flight Attendant:	*Of course! Anything else I can do for you?*
	¡Por supuesto! ¿Algo más que pueda hacer por usted?

Cris: *Yes, I am actually feeling a little sick.*

Sí. En verdad me siento un poco enferma.

Flight Attendant: *What are your symptoms?*

¿Cuáles son sus síntomas?

Cris: *I have a headache and a slight fever.*

Tengo dolor de cabeza y un poco de fiebre.

Flight Attendant: *Are you allergic to something?*

¿Es alérgica a algo?

Cris: *Only to aspirin.*

Solo a la aspirina.

Flight Attendant: *Ok. Please let me get help.*

Está bien. Por favor, permítame buscar ayuda.

Yes, I know. I picked the sick-person-talk for this practice. Can you blame me? I told you I made this book to be sure you would be completely prepared! Is your head better? No? Don't worry. We are landing now.

www.LearnLikeNatives.com

Chapter 3 – Looking for a Ride?

Welcome to your dream vacation! Only one thing stands between you and a strawberry daiquiri by the pool: you have to get to your hotel. This is how you really test your knowledge. Being already at your destination means your super-intensive-Spanish-camp is about to start. How fun is that?

First, let's begin with some basic words.

Taxi	Taxi
I need a **taxi**.	Necesito un **taxi**.

Same word? 1 point for globalization!

Shuttle	Transporte

Where can I get a **shuttle** to the Hilton Cartagena?	¿Dónde puedo tomar el **transporte** para el Hilton Cartagena?

Trans-poor-teh

"Transporte" is one of those basic and general words you will want to have on your menu. Anything from a cab to a rented car is a transportation method and is, therefore, a "transporte". Repeat with me: "trans-poor-teh".

Bus	Autobús
Where can I take a **bus** downtown?	¿Dónde puedo tomar un **autobús** al centro?

Please, remember the sound for a Spanish "u" is like an English "oo". Other than that, this should be an easy one.

Au-to-boos

If you are traveling with family, you are possibly thinking about driving around. We should take you to a car rental.

Rent a car	Alquilar un auto
I want to **rent a car**.	Quiero **alquilar un auto**.

Al-kee-lar un au-toh

To nail a Spanish "t" sound, it's always good to think of a British one. A strong, clear "t" that you can feel on the tip of your tongue.

Driver's license	Licencia de conducir
I will need a **driver's license**.	Voy a necesitar una **licencia de conducir**.

Li-sen-sia the con-doo-sir

You have finally arrived at your hotel. The landscape is beautiful and bright, decorated by the sound of palm trees blowing in the wind. Can you feel it? Great! I can too! But you got to get settled first. We are almost there.

www.LearnLikeNatives.com

Check in	Registrarme
I would like to **check into** my room.	Quisiera **registrarme** en mi habitación.

Have you been practicing your double "r"? I hope you have! Go with me:

Rre-his-trar-meh

Reservation	Reservación
Under whose name is the reservation?	¿A nombre de quién está la **reservación?**

Key	Llave
Here is your **key**.	Aquí está su **llave**.

Yah-veh

www.LearnLikeNatives.com

This is going to depend on what type of hotel you stay in. They now have keycards (tarjetas), or you can even access by pin code (código). Again, basic general words will save your life.

Elevator	Ascensor
Elevator is down the hall.	El **ascensor** se encuentra al final del pasillo.

Floor	Piso
Our room is on the 7th **floor.**	Nuestra habitación está en el 7mo **piso**.

This one sounds like "pee-soh".

Hey! I know you are eager to go into your room, so let's get in.

Look around your bedroom. You will find a bed, maybe a flat-screen, and a closet. You can see the sunset coming through your window behind some light shades. Let's make some necessary introductions.

Bed	Cama
Honey! Our **bed** is huge!	¡Cariño! Nuestra **cama** es enorme.

Kah-mah

TV	Televisor
Is it a smart **TV**?	¿Es un **televisor** inteligente?

The-le-vee-sor

Closet	Armario

I'll put the suitcases inside the **closet**.	Pondré las maletas dentro del **armario**.

Ar-mah-reeo

At this point, you should be truly acing those purring sounds. Go inside your bathroom. Tubs are not so common in the tropics, but you will definitely have a shower and a toilet. Given that bathrooms go with water, and water leaks, you want to pay attention to the following words and phrases in case you have to report any problems with the pipes.

Shower	Ducha
We have a massage **shower**.	Tenemos una **ducha** de masaje.

Doo-cha. I know what you are thinking, this sounds like another word I know. Keep in mind that in Spanish, the "ch" sound is similar to the "sh" one, but stronger--more to the tip of the tongue.

www.LearnLikeNatives.com

Toilet	Inodoro
Two bathrooms! We have a **toilet** each.	¡Dos baños! Cada uno tiene un **inodoro**.

Ee-no-tho-ro

Sink	Lavabo
I will put some things by the **sink**.	Voy a poner algunas cosas cerca del **lavabo**.

La-va-boh

Towels	Toalla
Hello! I need more **towels**.	¡Hola! Necesito más **toallas**.

Pillows	Almohadas

I also need 2 more **pillows**.	También necesito 2 **almohadas** más.

Practice these last two with me:

Toh-ah-yas

Al-moh-ah-das

It turns out my girlfriend uses four pillows and I always use extra towels. These two are basic survival for us.

Also, some hotels don't put mini-fridges inside the bedrooms anymore. In case you have any requests, follow me to the next phrase.

Mini fridge	Mini refrigerador
I would like a **mini-fridge** in my bedroom.	Me gustaría tener un **mini-refrigerador** en mi habitación.

You know the word for "mini". Let's practice the hard one:

Rre-fri-he-ra-dor

Mini-refrigerador

You have a nice bedroom in there! So, how about some practice?

Concierge: Hello! How can I help you?

¡Hola! ¿Cómo puedo ayudarle?

Dan: Hello! I think my sink is leaking.

¡Hola! Creo que mi lavamanos está goteando.

Concierge: I will send someone right away!

¡Enviaré a alguien enseguida!

Dan: Thanks. I appreciate your help.

Gracias. Aprecio tu ayuda.

Concierge: I am sorry for the inconvenience. Is there anything I can do to make your stay more pleasant?

Siento mucho los inconvenientes. ¿Hay algo que pueda hacer para que su estadía sea más placentera?

Dan: *Now that you mention it, I notice my room does not have a mini-fridge.*

Ahora que lo mencionas, noté que mi habitación no tiene mini-refrigerador.

Concierge: *Of course! Anything else?*

¡Claro! ¿Algo más?

Dan: *I'd like a couple more towels, and one extra pillow, please.*

Quisiera un par de toallas más, y una almohada extra, por favor.

Concierge: *Sure! Just in case you need more pillows, you have an extra inside the closet.*

¡Por supuesto! En caso de que necesitara más almohadas, hay una extra dentro del armario.

Dan: *Good to know! Thanks!*

¡Es bueno saberlo! ¡Gracias!

Concierge: *Is there anything else I can do for you today?*

¿Hay algo más que pueda hacer por usted el día de hoy?

Dan: *I am okay. Thank you very much.*

Estoy bien. Muchas gracias.

Concierge: *I will send help right away. Again, sorry for the inconvenience.*

Enviaré ayuda de inmediato. Nuevamente, me disculpo por los inconvenientes.

Dan: *It is all good. Thanks for your help.*

Está bien. Gracias por tu ayuda.

Concierge: *Thank you for being our guest!*

Gracias a usted por ser nuestro huésped.

Good! I think we are all set! Ready to go work on your tan?

www.LearnLikeNatives.com

Chapter 4 – I Find My Happiness Where the Sun Shines

You are finally here, in your dreamland. It is warm, and the sound of the ocean follows you all the way to your room. Far away, you hear some drums playing. This is all you wanted, and now you are ready to enjoy it. Aren't you? Let's check the weather for a second.

Weather	Clima
How's the **weather** in Colombia?	Cómo es el **clima** en Colombia?

First, just a quick check-up on the seasons.

Spring	Primavera
Flowers are blooming. **Spring** is here.	Las flores están floreciendo. Ha llegado la **primavera.**

Pree-ma-veh-ra

Summer	Verano
In the tropics, it always feels like **summer**.	En el trópico, siempre se siente como **verano**.

Be-rah-noh

Again, remember to work on your "open" vowels. The clearer, the better.

Fall	Otoño

| Look at the trees, and their **fall** colors. | Mira los árboles y sus colores de **otoño**. |

Oh-to-nio

As you know, the weather can surprise us. We know summer is supposed to be hot, and winter is cold, but so many other factors can add to it. Let's check some.

| Cloud | Nube |
| Look at that big **cloud**. | Mira esa gran **nube.** |

Noo-beh

| Sun | Sol |
| The **sun** was too strong. | El **sol** estaba muy fuerte. |

| Rain | Lluvia |

The **rain** came without a warning.	La **lluvia** vino sin avisar.

Yiu-veeah

Storm	Tormenta

Before we knew, the **storm** was here.	Antes de que supiéramos, la **tormenta** estaba aquí.

Thor-men-ta

Are any popular characters coming to mind? I bet there are!

Wind	Viento

The **wind** was so strong that the windows were moving.	El **viento** era tan fuerte que las ventanas se estaban moviendo.

Degrees	Grados
We were under 0 **degrees**.	Estábamos por debajo de 0 **grados**.

Grah-dos

Something to keep in mind is that the metric system is common outside the US. Depending on your destination, having a unit converter could be very useful.

Hurricane	Huracán
The **hurricane** wrecked it all.	El **huracán** lo destruyó todo.

Ooh-rah-can. It's the perfect word to practice your single "r" soft sound with.

Sunglasses	Lentes de sol

I left my **sunglasses** on the bed!	¡Dejé mis **lentes de sol** sobre la cama!

Lin-tes-the-sol

Hat	Sombrero
That's a nice **hat**!	¡Ese es un buen **sombrero**!

Som-breh-roh

This is a word many English speakers are used to hearing, which is great. Sombrero could generally stand for any kind of hat, including caps.

Sunscreen	Protector solar
Did you bring **sunscreen**?	Trajiste **protector solar**?

Pro-tek-tor so-lar

Umbrella	Sombrilla
Let's get under that **umbrella**.	Vamos a ponernos bajo esa **sombrilla**.

Sun-bree-ya

Raincoat	Impermeable
It is necessary to bring your **raincoat**.	Es necesario traer su **impermeable**.

In-per-meh-ah-bleh

This is a good word. "Impermeable" is the Spanish word for waterproof, so it is something to keep in mind when you go shopping.

Talking about shopping, why don't we go for a little spree?

Seller: *Hello! Good afternoon. How can I help you?*

¡Hola! Buenas tardes. ¿Cómo puedo ayudarle?

Ken: *Hey! Good afternoon. I would like to buy some things.*

¡Hola! Buenas tardes. Me gustaría comprar algunas cosas.

Seller: *Sure! What do you have in mind?*

¡Seguro! ¿Qué tiene en mente?

Ken: *Everything. I need an umbrella, sunglasses, a raincoat... everything.*

Todo. Necesito una sombrilla, lentes de sol, un impermeable... todo.

Seller: *Oh, I see. Did the hurricane catch you off guard?*

Oh, ya veo. ¿El huracán le tomó por sorpresa?

Ken: *Yes. Totally. It's been crazy. Sun goes and rain comes. Repeatedly.*

Sí. Totalmente. Ha sido una locura. El sol se va y viene la lluvia. Repetidamente

Seller: I am sorry to hear that. I will help you, gladly.

Siento escuchar eso. Le ayudaré, con mucho gusto.

Ken: Thanks! What raincoats do you have?

¡Gracias! ¿Cuáles impermeables tienes?

Seller: I have these raincoats. Good quality and they protect you down to 0 degrees.

Tengo estos impermeables. Buena calidad y le protege hasta los 0 grados.

Ken: Awesome! What about umbrellas?

¡Genial! ¿Cuáles sombrillas tienes?

Seller: I have many. It depends on what size you are looking for.

Tengo muchas. Depende de qué tamaño busca.

Ken: *Just a couple of small umbrellas. Something easy to carry.*

Solo un par de sombrillas pequeñas. Algo que sea fácil de cargar.

Seller: *Sure! Why don't you come with me to pick sunglasses?*

¡Por supuesto! ¿Por qué no me acompaña a elegir lentes de sol?

Ken: *Glad to! I will follow you.*

¡Encantando! Te sigo.

Seller: *Very well. This way, please.*

Muy bien. Por acá, por favor.

I hope you have sunscreen. The rain is finally gone, so we are going to some touristy places in a while, and I do not want you to get a nasty sunburn. Remember to bring all of your equipment. As always, the most important thing is to be prepared.

Chapter 5 – I Have So Many Stories to Tell You

Do you know what I love most about life in general? The stories! And this is especially true for traveling because it is all about learning new cultures, meeting new and different people, and facing things you never thought you would.

I remember being in this beautiful colonial place in Queretaro, Mexico. Everything looked perfect. The location was terrific; it was close to all the tourist attractions, and the architecture in our hotel was breathtakingly beautiful. The price was good. Everything was perfect… until I got to my room and found my toilet was inside the shower.

Trust me. I am not picky. I decided to stay there for the night because the location was amazing and the hotel had already been paid for. I have to admit, though, that all optimism vanished after I went to the bathroom in the middle of the night and got my socks wet from the shower. Needless to say, it was a GREAT and funny story to tell my friends and one of those things I will remember forever.

If you are a storyteller, as I am, then you need a few more tools so you can delight your friends–even your newest local friends—with the fantastic things you have gone through. For that, we will use two different verbal forms to help you bring your story to life. You know this, or at least you may have heard of it back in school. Don't worry. We promised no grammar, okay? I want to show you some examples.

First, let's go through the first one: past simple, which in Spanish, we call "pretérito indefinido". It is close to "undefined past", something great for grammar and AWFUL for blind dates.

Regular verbs in Spanish can have 1 of 3 terminations: -ar (as in "viajar"), -er (as in "comer") and -ir (as in "descubrir"). This is important because, as you will see, once you can spot the termination of the verb, you will be able to figure out all conjugations without memorizing them.

For practical uses, we will group 3rd person pronouns as singular. "He", "she", and "it" will form a group.

We'll start with a verb we know: "viajar" – to travel.

To travel	Viajar	Root	Termination
I traveled	Yo viajé	Viaj-	Ar changes to "é"

You traveled	Tú viajaste		Ar changes to "aste"
He/She/It traveled	Él/Ella/Eso viajó		Ar changes to "ó"
We traveled	Nosotros viajamos		Ar changes to "amos"
You traveled	Ustedes viajaron		Ar changes to "aron"
They traveled	Ellos/Ellas viajaron		Ar changes to "aron"

Do you see what we did there? For conjugating regular verbs, you need to spot the root of the verb and then shift the termination, according to each case. For the verb "viajar", the root is "viaj-". For the verb "gustar" (to like), the root is "gust-". And for the verb "formar" (to form), we have to employ the root "form-".

The same thing will happen for the group of verbs ending in "er", as in "comer" (root "com-") or "sorprender" (root "sorprend-"), and for the "ir" termination group, as in "hundir" (root "hund-") or "compartir" (root "compart-").

Come on! It may look hard, but it is not really that awful. You just need some practice and a few pointers, like the ones we discussed.

Let's go for a quick practice.

I traveled to Spain last year.	Yo viajé a España el año pasado.
She traveled through the entire continent.	Ella viajó a través de todo el continente.
You traveled a lot the last two months.	Ustedes viajaron bastante los últimos dos meses.
We traveled to Mexico during the summer.	Nosotros viajamos a México durante el verano.

Can you see it? In every sentence, all the actions have already happened: last year, last summer, the last two months. Past perfect is for things in the past. Let's keep checking on this with the second termination, "er".

To eat	Comer	Root	Termination
I ate	Yo comí	Com-	Er changes to "í"
You ate	Tú comiste		Er changes to "iste"
He/She/It ate	Él/Ella/Eso comió		Er changes to "ió"
We ate	Nosotros comimos		Er changes to "imos"
You ate	Ustedes comieron		Er changes to "ieron"

They ate	Ellos/Ellas comieron		Er changes to "ieron"

Let's practice with some sentences.

You ate the entire cake.	Tú comiste todo el pastel.
She ate only a piece of cake.	Ella comió solo un pedazo de pastel.
We ate one piece each.	Nosotros comimos un pedazo cada uno.
They ate the rest of the cake.	Ellos comieron el resto del pastel.

This is important for stories–you have to eat. Also, as seen, it is a good verb to help solve some family culinary disputes.

To discover	**Descubrir**	**Root**	**Termination**
I discovered	Yo descubrí	Descubr-	Ir changes to "í"

You discovered	Tú descubriste		Ir changes to "íste"
He/She/It discovered	Él/Ella/Eso descubrió		Ir changes to "ió"
We discovered	Nosotros descubrimos		Ir changes to "imos"
You discovered	Ustedes descubrieron		Ir changes to "ieron"
They discovered	Ellos/Ellas descubrieron		Ir changes to "ieron"

Are you getting closer? Let's go for some practice.

You discovered a new way.	Tú descubriste una nueva manera.
He discovered his present.	Él descubrió su regalo.
You discovered a mark under the door.	Ustedes descubrieron una marca bajo la puerta.
They discovered that there was no door.	Ellos descubrieron que no había una puerta.

As we discussed earlier, for all regular verbs ending in "er", you only have to find the root and then add the termination for the conjugation you want.

How are you doing so far? Don't worry. We will keep working on this a little longer, using more examples.

Our next verb is "to have". "To have" and "to be" are fundamental in building complex sentences, but they are also on the list of irregular verbs for English and Spanish, so the changes we described earlier will not work for these verbs. Let's take a look.

To have	Tener
I had	Yo tuve
You had	Tú tuviste
He/She/It had	Él/Ella/Eso tuvo
We had	Nosotros tuvimos
You had	Ustedes tuvieron

| They had | Ellos/Ellas tuvieron |

Do you want to go for some practice?

I had such a great night. It was magical.	Yo tuve una gran noche. Fue mágica.
You had everything you asked for.	Tú tuviste todo lo que pediste.
She had a beautiful dress.	Ella tenía un hermoso vestido.
We had so much to be grateful.	Nosotros tuvimos mucho que agradecer.

The next verb is a little more complex and kind of philosophic—it is the verb "to be". For English, as well as for Spanish, it is the verb of existence. It turns out, in Spanish it translates to two different verbs: the verb "ser" and the verb "estar". Let's see how this works.

To be	Ser	Estar
I was	Yo fui	Yo estuve
You were	Tú fuiste	Tú estuviste
He/She/It was	Él/Ella/Eso fue	Él/Ella/Eso estuvo
We were	Nosotros fuimos	Nosotros estuvimos
You were	Ustedes fueron	Ustedes estuvieron
They were	Ellos/Ellas fueron	Ellos/Ellas estuvieron

You may be wondering: when should I use what?

The verb "ser" applies to the following cases:

- When defining or identifying someone or something. For example: "Ese fue Juan." – "That was Juan."; "Ustedes fueron soldados." – "You were soldiers."
- When describing someone's or something's characteristics. As in, "Tú fuiste muy hermosa." – "You

were so beautiful." Or, "Ellos fueron muy rápidos." – "They were really quick."

- When speaking of the weather, the time of the day, and similar topics. "Eso fue en el otoño." – "It was in the autumn."; "Eso fue alrededor de las cuatro de la tarde." – "It was around four in the afternoon."
- When locating an event. "La fiesta fue en casa de Natalia." – "The party was at Natalia's house.; "La cumbre fue en San Francisco." – "The Summit was in San Francisco."

On the other side, the verb "estar" applies for these cases:

- When locating people and things in space. "Yo estuve en California." – "I was in California."; "Ellos estuvieron en la casa todo el tiempo." – "They were at home all the time."
- When speaking of someone's or something's state. "Ella estuvo sola todo el tiempo." – "She was alone all the time."; "Ellos estuvieron desordenados." – "They were messy."

First, a quick practice with the conjugations for "ser".

| *I was so happy that night.* | Yo fui tan feliz aquella noche. |

She was Prom Queen.	Ella fue Reina del Baile.
We were young once.	Nosotros fuimos jóvenes una vez.
They were invincible.	Ellos fueron invencibles.

Are you feeling good about this one? Let's go for "estar".

I was there all night.	Yo estuve ahí toda la noche.
He was busy that night.	Él estuvo ocupado esa noche.
We were by the pool.	Nosotros estuvimos junto a la piscina.
They were M.I.A.	Ellos estuvieron perdidos en acción.

As with any other language, Spanish is all about structure, and I promise it will get easier with some practice. As always, I will point other practical uses for this tense through the dialogue.

I said before, I was going to make a revision through two verbal forms. First was the undefined past. As you may have noticed, undefined past actions have already happened.

On the other side, in sentences using the imperfect past, you never know when the action started or ended. It's the equivalent to say that "you used to" do something. You know it's not happening anymore, but can't really tell when it ended. With this being said, let's see some examples using the same verbs as before.

To travel	Viajar	Root	Termination
I traveled	Yo viajaba	Viaj-	Ar changes to "aba"
You traveled	Tú viajabas		Ar changes to "abas"
He/She/It traveled	Él/Ella/Eso viajaba		Ar changes to "aba"

We traveled	Nosotros viajábamos		Ar changes to "ábamos"
You traveled	Ustedes viajaban		Ar changes to "aban"
They traveled	Ellos/Ellas viajaban		Ar changes to "aban"

Bee-ah-ha-ba; bee-ah-ha-bas; bee-ah-ha-bah-mos; bee-ah-ha-ban

I traveled all the time, until I lost my passport.	Yo viajaba todo el tiempo, hasta que perdí mi pasaporte.
She traveled the continent while he was getting his degree.	Ella viajaba el continente, mientras él estaba obteniendo su título.
You traveled before having kids.	Ustedes viajaban antes de tener a los niños.

| We traveled every two months. | Nosotros viajábamos cada dos meses. |

Notice how in these last sentences, you could have used "used to travel" instead of "traveled". This is important because it works as a hint—every time you can change an English verb in the past tense for a "used to + verb", you are in the presence of Spanish imperfect past, and therefore all changes apply as we just practiced.

I used to travel all the time until I lost my passport.	Yo viajaba todo el tiempo, hasta que perdí mi pasaporte.
She used to travel the continent, while he was getting his degree.	Ella viajaba el continente, mientras él estaba obteniendo su título.
You used to travel before having kids.	Ustedes viajaban antes de tener a los niños.

www.LearnLikeNatives.com

We used to travel every two months.	Nosotros viajábamos cada dos meses.

Are you getting better with your phrasing? Let's keep working.

To eat	**Comer**	**Root**	**Termination**
I ate	Yo comía		Er changes to "ía"
You ate	Tú comías		Er changes to "ías"
He/She/It ate	Él/Ella/Eso comía	Com-	Er changes to "ía"
We ate	Nosotros comíamos		Er changes to "íamos"
You ate	Ustedes comían		Er changes to "ían"

www.LearnLikeNatives.com

They ate	Ellos/Ellas comían		Er changes to "ían"

As always, don't worry. Practice makes perfect, and in no time, you will have each tense covered. Let's keep practicing.

You ate an entire cake while I was watching TV.	Tú comías un pastel mientras yo veía la televisión.
She ate one piece of cake after dinner every night.	Ella comía un pedazo de pastel luego de la cena, cada noche.
We ate one piece every time we saw each other.	Nosotros comíamos un pedazo, cada vez que nos veíamos.
That night, they ate with so much joy!	¡Esa noche, ellos comían con tanta alegría!

How is this sounding to you? Is it making any sense? Let's see more verbs.

www.LearnLikeNatives.com

To discover	Descubrir	Root	Termination
I discovered	Yo descubría	Descubr-	Ir changes to "ía"
You discovered	Tú descubrías		Ir changes to "ías"
He/She/It discovered	Él/Ella/Eso descubría		Ir changes to "ía"
We discovered	Nosotros descubríamos		Ir changes to "íamos"
You discovered	Ustedes descubrían		Ir changes to "ían"
They discovered	Ellos/ellas descubrían		Ir changes to "ían"

Can you see how the terminations shift? Let's see some examples.

I discovered new ways, before that happened.	Yo descubría nuevas formas, antes de que eso sucediera.
You discovered new ways to surprise me, night after night.	Tú descubrías nuevas formas de sorprenderme, noche tras noche.

She discovered a mark, and then another.	Ella descubría una marca, y luego otra.
They discovered what happened, until you found out.	Ellos descubrían qué sucedía, hasta que tú te enteraste.

See? It can get easier, quick. Let's go to our next verb: the irregular "to have", or "tener".

To have	**Tener**
I had	Yo tenía
You had	Tú tenías
He/She/It had	Él/Ella/Eso tenía
We had	Nosotros teníamos
You had	Ustedes tenían

| They had | Ellos/Ellas tenían |

Teh-nee-ah; teh-nee-us; teh-nee-ah-mos; teh-ní-an

I had everything I could wish.	Yo tenía todo lo que podía desear.
She had every opportunity.	Ella tenía todas las oportunidades.
You had other plans, and it worked.	Tú tenías otros planes, y funcionó.
We had so much to do.	Nosotros teníamos mucho por hacer.

Pay attention to the next verb. The verb "to be" is also an option when building sentences that are more complex. This turns it into a necessary tool to have in order to tell a great story.

To be	Ser	Estar
I was	Yo era	Yo estaba
You were	Tú eras	Tú estabas
He/She/It was	Él/Ella/Eso era	Él/Ella/Eso estaba
We were	Nosotros éramos	Nosotros estábamos
You were	Ustedes eran	Ustedes estaban
They were	Ellos/Ellas eran	Ellos/Ellas estaban

Es-tah-bah; es-tah-bas; es-tah-bah-mos; es-tah-ban

Let's practice a bit more.

I was a Prom Queen.	Yo era Reina del Baile.
He was a great athlete.	Él era un gran atleta.

We were a great team.	Nosotros éramos un gran equipo.
They were invincible.	Ellos eran invencibles.

Now that we have gone through the verbs "to have" and "to be" in the past tense, we can build on some more complex tenses.

We have the "pretérito anterior". First, let me give an example:

When it had finished raining, I kept walking.

As you can see, you combine "had" ("have" in the past tense) with another regular verb in past participle to indicate two actions that are finished with, one after the other.

In Spanish, that structure remains.

Cuando hubo terminado de llover, seguí caminando.

I understand you may be a little confused now. Do not rush. Let's see some more examples.

When he had awakened, she was already gone.	Cuando él hubo despertado, ella ya se había ido.
Once they had found the ball, they came back to play.	Cuando ellos hubieron encontrado la bola, volvieron a jugar.
As soon as I had studied, I took five minutes for myself.	Tan pronto hube estudiado, tomé cinco minutos para mí.

Through our dialogue, you will have the chance to see how all these elements fit together.

Kate: Hello! I am so glad you came back from your trip.

¡Hola! Estoy muy alegre de que hayas regresado de tu viaje.

Alex: Hi! I am glad as well. It was a fun trip.

¡Hola! Yo también estoy contento. Fue un viaje gracioso.

Kate: *Great! Tell me!*

¡Genial! Cuéntame.

Alex: *Remember how I used to love rain?*

¿Recuerdas cómo me encantaba la lluvia?

Kate: *Of course.*

Por supuesto.

Alex: *It turns out it was raining in Puebla, but I had bought tickets to see a movie.*

Resulta que estaba lloviendo en Puebla, pero había comprado boletos para ver una película.

Kate: *Such a pity!*

¡Que pena!

Alex: *I have always had that thing with rain.*

Siempre he tenido esa cosa con la lluvia.

Kate: *Indeed.*

Efectivamente.

Do you feel like an expert at putting phrases together? You should. We have come a long way. Besides, you are going to need those skills now because we are going on an adventure.

www.LearnLikeNatives.com

Chapter 6 – So Many Roads and So Many Places

I personally love to walk. Being younger, and single, I would put my earphones in and walk through any new city I got the chance to visit. When with my girlfriend, I put the earphones away and we enjoy long chats while walking and looking around. Sometimes she takes pictures, and they are mostly of me taking pictures of her, or the landscape. But I so enjoy watching her under all the diverse shades and lights. Have you ever noticed how every city has different colors and vibes?

Back to business. Tell me: what do you typically want to visit first when exploring a new city? Wherever you want to go, I am here to help you. Why don't we start with a few basics?

Museum	Museo
Where is the Prado **Museum**?	¿Dónde está el **Museo** del Prado?

Moo-se-oh

www.LearnLikeNatives.com

The first syllable is easy. Just think of the sound a cow makes, "moooo-seh-oh".

Square	Plaza
How can I get to Santo Domingo **Square**?	Cómo puedo llegar a la **Plaza** Santo Domingo?

Pla-za

Avenue	Avenida
What can I find on Alameda **avenue**?	¿Qué puedo encontrar en la **avenida** Alameda?

Ah-veh-nee-da

This one should not be a problem. The pronunciation is very similar to "avenue".

Monuments	Monumentos
Peru is rich in history and **monuments.**	Perú es rico en historia y **monumentos.**

Moh-noo-men-tos

Park	Parque
Park Güell is in Barcelona.	El **Parque** Güell está en Barcelona.

Par-ke

Church	Iglesia
They gave me this **church** as a reference.	Me dieron esta **iglesia** como referencia.

Ee-gle-si-a

Not to be unholy, but traveling is not just about history and great buildings. It is also about having fun and experiencing the true local culture, such as going to bars and clubs.

Bar	Bar
Where is this **bar**?	¿Dónde está ese **bar**?

See? Globalization scores again!

Now that you know some places, let's take you to them.

Across	Cruzando
You can find them **across** the avenue.	Puedes encontrarlos **cruzando** la avenida.

This should be a piece of cake. Say, "cruise" (like the boat) and add "ando" at the end.

In front of	Delante de
He is waiting **in front of** the statue.	Él está esperando **delante de** la estatua.

Deh-lant-te-de

Opposite	Opuesto
We were walking in the **opposite** direction.	Estábamos caminando en la dirección **opuesta.**

Oh-poo-es-tah

www.LearnLikeNatives.com

Street	Calle
You can find it down the **street**.	Puedes encontrarlo al final de la **calle**.

Ka-ye

Blocks	Cuadras
How many **blocks** are left?	¿Cuántas **cuadras** nos faltan?

Ku-ah-dras

Subway	Subterráneo
We can get there by **subway**.	Podemos llegar a través del **subterráneo**.

Ready for this one? Sub-te-rra-neo.

Mall	Centro comercial

| What kind of **mall** would you like to visit? | ¿Qué tipo de **centro comercial** te gustaría visitar? |

Cen-tro ko-mer-sial

| Recommend | Recomendar |
| What can you **recommend?** | ¿Qué me puedes **recomendar?** |

Re-co-men-dar

"Recomendar" is a general word for "suggestions". So, whenever you are out of ideas, just remember this one.

In terms of tourism, you should already be an expert at getting around. You have learned how to request a cab, rent a car, and ask for directions and recommendations. You are almost done with this section, so why don't we practice a little more?

Front desk (Recepción): *Hello! How can I help you?*

¡Hola! ¿Cómo puedo ayudarle?

Allen: I would like some recommendations for places to visit.

Me gustarían algunas recomendaciones de lugares para visitar.

Front desk: Very well. What type of place did you have in mind? A club, a museum?

Muy bien. ¿Qué clase de lugar tiene en mente? ¿Un club, un museo...?

Allen: I have heard that you have beautiful squares and monuments in this city.

He escuchado que tienen hermosas plazas y monumentos en esta ciudad.

Front desk: That is true. Sadly, most cultural attractions are across town.

Eso es cierto. Lamentablemente, la mayoría de las atracciones culturales está cruzando la ciudad.

Philip: Oh, I see. Could you give me some directions, please?

Oh, ya veo. ¿Podría darme algunas direcciones, por favor?

Front desk: Sure! Would you like to travel by car or take the subway?

¡Claro! ¿Le gustaría viajar en auto o tomar el subterráneo?

Philip: I would rather take a subway and walk.

Prefiero tomar el subterráneo y caminar.

Front desk: Very well. The subway is only 3 blocks away.

Muy bien. El subterráneo se encuentra a solo 3 cuadras.

Philip: Perfect! How do I get there?

¡Perfecto! ¿Cómo llego hasta allá?

Front desk: *You only have to go down this street, take a right, and walk straight for 3 blocks.*

Solo tiene que caminar hasta el final de la calle, doblar a la derecha y caminar recto durante 3 cuadras.

Philip: *That sounds easy. Thank you very much!*

Eso suena fácil. ¡Muchísimas gracias!

Front desk: *All right, then. After you get to the subway, go to the mainline and take a train to Baquedano station.*

Muy bien, entonces. Luego de llegar al subterráneo, vaya a la línea principal y tome un tren a la estación Baquedano.

Philip: *Very good. I appreciate your help.*

Muy bien. Aprecio su ayuda.

Front desk: *My pleasure. Have a nice day.*

Un placer. Que tenga un lindo día.

Allen: *Likewise. Bye.*

Igualmente. Adiós.

Ready to walk and get lost in new cities? I bet you are eager to do it. You better get dressed, go out, enjoy, and gather all the amazing stories you can!

I am feeling a little hungry, though. What do you say? Should we go and grab a bite?

Chapter 7 – Eat, Travel, Love

Food is one of my favorite parts of traveling. Eating is an awesome way to learn a bit more about the culture and history of each place. Your nose and tongue become guides that can lead you through unknown passages, allowing you to enjoy the aromas of Chile in a glass of cabernet; or the Mexican spice in a dish of mole poblano; or to experience the culinary revolution in Peru, in the shape of a sweet and sour mango ceviche. Flavors are unique everywhere you go, and that is what makes them a huge part of traveling.

For this reason, I want to be sure I am giving you the opportunity to have the best experience ever. Plus, ordering food is a recurrent activity, which means you will have many chances to practice. I can also assure you something: some of the best typical food places will not have a translator. With that in mind, let's start this chapter.

Restaurant	Restaurante
Let's go into that **restaurant.**	Vamos a entrar a ese **restaurante.**

Rehs-taoo-ran-teh

It is very similar to the English word, yet remember to put emphasis on the open vowels.

Table	Mesa
Table for 4, please.	**Mesa** para 4, por favor.

Meh-sa

Suggestions	Sugerencias
Do you want to hear today's **suggestions**?	¿Quieren escuchar las **sugerencias** de hoy?

Suh-he-ren-sias

Portion	Ración
I want a **portion** of fries.	Quiero una **ración** de papas fritas.

Rah-seeon

www.LearnLikeNatives.com

This is becoming easier with time, huh?

Fork	Tenedor
I dropped my **fork.**	Dejé caer mi **tenedor.**

Teh-neh-door

Spoon	Cuchara
Can I get a **spoon**?	Puedes darme una **cuchara**?

Cu-cha-ra

Do you remember this sound? Put it in the top of your tongue, so the "ch" will be stronger.

Knife	Cuchillo
I will need a meat **knife.**	Necesitaré un **cuchillo** para carnes.

Cu-chi-yo

Plate	Plato
Can you bring an extra **plate**?	¿Puedes traer un **plato** extra?

Appetizer	Entrada
Do you want an **appetizer**?	¿Quieres una **entrada**?

N-tra-da

"Entrada" is a good word because it translates both as an appetizer and as an entry. So, if ever looking for an entry, remember: "n-tra-da".

Main dish	Plato principal
For the **main dish**, I want the chicken.	Como **plato principal**, quiero el pollo.

Okay, we already practiced "plato" when learning "plate". "Plato" can mean both the instrument, as well as the actual food when speaking of a type of dish.

Pla-toh-preen-si-pal

Well-cooked	Bien cocido
I want my steak **well-cooked.**	Quiero mi bisteck **bien cocido.**

Bee-n ko-si-doh

Bee-n means "good".

Medium	Término medio
Medium is fine for me.	**Término medio** está bien para mí.

Tehr-mee-no-meh-dee-o

Dessert	Postre

| Of course, I want a **dessert.** | Por supuesto, quiero un **postre.** |

Pus-treh

| Vegan | Vegano |
| Do you have a vegan menu? | ¿Tiene menú **vegano**? |

Beh-gah-no

| Check | Cuenta |
| I want my **check**, please. | Quiero mi **cuenta**, por favor. |

Quen-tah

Are you excited to order your first dish? Why don't we go to practice a bit more before...

Waiter (mesonero): *Good afternoon! Welcome to our restaurant. My name is Shawn. How many are you?*

| | ¡Buenas tardes! Bienvenidos a nuestro restaurante. Mi nombre es Shawn. ¿Cuántos son ustedes? |

Mike: *Hello! We have a reservation under Paulson. Table for 4.*

¡Hola! Tenemos una reservación a nombre de Paulson. Mesa para 4.

Waiter: *Yes, here you are. Come with me, please.*

Sí, aquí están. Vengan conmigo, por favor.

Mike: *I would like to order right away. We are starving.*

Quisiera ordenar de inmediato. Estamos muriendo de hambre.

Waiter: *Perfect. What would you like to order?*

Perfecto. ¿Qué desean ordenar?

Mike: *What are your suggestions?*

¿Cuáles son tus sugerencias?

Waiter: *The lobster ceviche as an appetizer. For the main dish, we have a causa accompanied by a saffron sauce.*

El ceviche de langosta como entrada. Como plato principal, tenemos una Causa acompañada de salsa de azafrán.

Mike: *Sounds great! I want one of each. Also, a salad and two beef dishes.*

¡Suena fabuloso! Quiero uno de cada uno. Además, quiero una ensalada y dos platos de carne.

Waiter: *Do you want extra plates to share?*

¿Quieren platos extra para compartir?

Mike: Yes, please.

Sí, por favor.

Waiter:	*Perfect. I will be back in a second with your plates, forks, and meat knives.*
	Perfecto. Volveré en un segundo con sus platos, tenedores y cuchillos de carne.
Mike:	*Thank you very much.*
	Muchas gracias.
Waiter:	*I'll be right back.*
	Volveré de inmediato.

I bet this chapter was easy. How did you feel after repeating that last dialogue? Look... I do not want to freak you out, but you are about to feel a bit under the weather.

www.LearnLikeNatives.com

Chapter 8 – Sick & Abroad!

Every time I travel abroad, I buy insurance, but the truth is I always hope I will not need it. Being sick can be scary, and no one likes to feel ill. Moreover, nobody wants it to interrupt their vacation! However, if you have to be prepared for something, this is definitely it. Great communication can be the key to solving major problems. So, let's get prepared.

Ill	Enfermo
I think I am **ill**.	Creo que estoy **enfermo**.

Here we see the word "n-ferh-moh" again, I know, but it is very important.

Cold	Resfriado
I think I caught a **cold**.	Creo que cogí un **resfriado**.

Rehs-free-ah-doh

Cough	Tos
I have a slight **cough.**	Tengo un poco de **tos.**

Tos

Pain	Dolor
I took something for the **pain.**	Me tomé algo para el **dolor.**

Doh-lohr

Practice those wide-open "o" sounds.

Migraine	Migraña
I have a **migraine.**	Tengo **migraña.**

Mee-grah-nia

Swollen	Hinchado

| My throat is a bit **swollen.** | Mi garganta está un poco **hinchada.** |

In-cha-dah

| Call the doctor | Llamar al médico |
| Do you want to call the **doctor**? | ¿Quieres llamar al **médico**? |

Meh-dee-ko

Hearing the word "médico" can work as an emergency signal. Please, practice this one.

Meh-dee-ko

| Emergency | Emergencia |
| I have an **emergency.** | Tengo una **emergencia.** |

Eh-mer-hen-sia

| Feel | Siento |

I **feel** a bit better.	Me **siento** un poco mejor.

See-N-to

Patient	Paciente
I am a **patient** of Dr. Castillo.	Soy un **paciente** del Dr. Castillo.

Pah-See-N-teh

Blood pressure	Presión sanguínea
The **blood pressure** is fine.	La **presión sanguínea** está bien.

Preh-si-on san-ghee-ne-ah

Pharmacy	Farmacia
Where is the nearest **pharmacy**?	¿Dónde está la **farmacia** más cercana?

Similar to English: "phar-ma-cee-ah".

Prescription	Prescripción
I will need a **prescription.**	Voy a necesitar una **prescripción.**

Pres-krip-sion

Pills	Píldoras
How many **pills** do I need?	¿Cuántas **píldoras** necesito?

Peel-doh-rahs

We already did something similar to this in the airplane chapter, remember? So, as I have been saying, this knowledge is additive. You know English. You have done this before. You got it. Ready for practice?

Liam: *Hello! I would like to speak to Dr. Castillo.*

Hola! Me gustaría hablar con el Dr. Castillo.

Secretary (secretaria): *Good afternoon, sir. What is your name?*

Buenas tardes, señor. ¿Cuál es su nombre?

Liam: *I am Liam Smith. One of his patients.*

Soy Liam Smith. Uno de sus pacientes.

Secretary: *Good afternoon, sir. Why do you call today?*

¿Cuál es el motivo de su llamada?

Liam: *I have an emergency. My youngest son has a strong headache.*

Tengo una emergencia. Mi hijo menor tiene un fuerte dolor de cabeza.

Secretary: *Any other symptoms?*

Algún otro síntoma?

Liam: *38°C fever. Also complaints of abdominal pain.*

Fiebre de 38°C. También se queja de dolor abdominal.

Secretary: *Is he allergic to something?*

¿Es alérgico a algo?

Liam: *Yes. To gluten.*

Sí. Al gluten.

Secretary: *Is he taking any prescriptions?*

¿Está tomando alguna prescripción?

Liam: *No, just a dietary supplement.*

No. Sólo un suplemento dietético.

Secretary: *Come here at once and bring those pills.*

Vengan aquí de inmediato y traigan esas píldoras.

Yeah, I know what you are thinking: no parent with a celiac kid would give him random pills! I feel you, but I have also seen it happen.

I truly hope my book is helping you. I am a travel and diversity lover, and I hope other people enjoy these experiences just as much. I know how much independence and confidence you can get by being able to communicate in more than one language. So, stay with me! We need you focused and optimistic! Did not I tell you? We need to go find you a job.

Chapter 9 – Learn the Ropes

Looking for new employment can be both a frustrating and an exciting situation. I am used to working on my own—which allows me to travel more—but I still have to get my own clients. If you are relocating or just thinking of spending a season in another city, finding a job at a local business could be a great opportunity to get in touch with the culture from a closer perspective.

As always, I will try to keep it simple.

Employment	Empleo
I am looking for **employment.**	Estoy buscando **empleo.**

M-pleh-oh

Employer	Jefe
My **employer** looks nice.	Mi **jefe** se ve agradable.

The most direct translation for "employer" is "empleador", but it is not very common to hear people say it that way.

He-feh

Employee	Empleado
I am an **employee** of this shop.	Soy un **empleado** de esta tienda.

M-pleh-ah-doh

Permanent position	Puesto fijo
I would like a **permanent position**.	Quisiera un **puesto fijo**.

Pooes-to-fee-jo

Temporary job	Trabajo temporal
I have a **temporary job**.	Tengo un **trabajo temporal**.

Trah-bah-joh-tem-po-rahl

www.LearnLikeNatives.com

Salary	Sueldo
I want a **salary** increase.	Quiero un aumento de **sueldo**.

Again, "salario" is the direct equivalent, but in terms of pronunciation and use, "sueldo" will perfectly do the work.

First and last name are very common expressions, and so far, you must have used it a dozen times. However, we will need it to write your CV, so just in case…

First name	Nombre
What is your **first name**?	¿Cuál es tu primer **nombre**?

Nom-bre

Last name	Apellido
My **last name** is Lopez.	Mi **apellido** es Lopez.

Ah-peh-yi-doh

Profession	Profesión
What is your **profession**?	¿Cuál es tu **profesión**?

Pro-phe-sion

Credentials	Credenciales
Here are my **credentials**.	Aquí están mis **credenciales.**

Kre-den-sia-les

Skills	Habilidades
These are my main **skills**.	Estas son mis **habilidades** principales.

Ah-bee-lee-da-des

As we know, the hiring criteria is changing. For many companies around the world, professions and studies are not as important as they used to be. Therefore, a very complete list of your most prominent skills will be important.

Job title	Título profesional
My **job title** is Manager.	Mi **título profesional** es Gerente.

Tee-too-loh-pro-phe-sio-nal

Job description	Descripción de rol
That is not under my **job description**.	Eso no está dentro de mi **descripción de rol**.

Des-krip-cion-the-rol

Your job description is, of course, crucial. While your job title might say something, your job description should provide a specific idea of what is expected from you.

Milestone	Hito
What is your favorite **milestone?**	¿Cuál es tu **hito** preferido?

Ee-toh

www.LearnLikeNatives.com

As you may know, where you have worked in the past and for how long are not as important anymore. What truly matters is what you got to accomplish while working with this or that during that time. Select your "hitos" to show for your skills.

Manager	Gerente
Congratulations! You are the new **manager.**	¡Felicidades! Eres el nuevo **gerente.**

N-kar-ga-doh

Congratulations! I am so happy for you!

That escalated quickly, huh?

You know my motto: practice makes perfect! Let's dive into our next dialogue.

Manager (gerente): *Hello! What can I do for you?*

¡Hola! ¿Qué puedo hacer por ti?

Owen: *Hello! I am looking for employment.*

¡Hola! Estoy buscando trabajo.

Manager What is your name?

¿Cuál es tu nombre?

Owen: Owen Miller.

Owen Miller.

Manager Very well. What type of work are you looking for?

Muy bien. ¿Qué clase de trabajo estás buscando?

Owen: I would like anything. Even a temporary job.

Me gustaría cualquier cosa. Incluso un trabajo temporal.

Manager Right. Did you bring your CV?

Correcto. ¿Trajiste tu CV?

Owen: Yes. Here it is.

Sí. Aquí está.

Manager Very good. What are your major skills?

Muy bien. ¿Cuáles son tu mayores habilidades?

Owen: I am good at logo design.

Soy bueno en diseño de logos.

Manager What are your most relevant milestones from the past year?

¿Cuáles son sus hitos más importantes del último año?

Owen: I won campaigns for logo refreshments in 5 major companies.

Gané campañas para refrescar el logo de 5 grandes empresas.

Manager	*All right. We will call you for another interview.*
	Muy bien. Te llamaremos para otra entrevista.
Owen:	*Do you have any vacancies?*
	¿Tienen ustedes alguna vacante?
Manager	*We have a job for a designer. It could turn into a permanent position.*
	Tenemos trabajo para un diseñador. Puede convertirse en un trabajo fijo.
Owen:	*That is great.*
	Eso es genial.
Manager	*Yes, it is. You would get an entry salary plus bonuses.*
	Sí, lo es. Obtendrías salario de entrada más bonos.

www.LearnLikeNatives.com

Owen: *Awesome. I will wait for your call.*

Increíble. Esperaré su llamada.

We have already had a little walkthrough for an interview, but we will work harder on that in the next chapter. After all, we have to get you ready for your first big job.

www.LearnLikeNatives.com

Chapter 10 – Bring, Learn & Lead

As the title for this chapter suggests, now is the time to bring, to learn, and to lead, because you have to shine in your job interview. For this, we will work in a new tense: the future. This is the moment to talk about ambition, show how good you are at planning and projecting, and demonstrate why you know you will be a great fit.

First verb: "to bring" – "aportar". As you will see, the root is "aport-".

Ah-por-tar

To bring	Aportar	Root	Termination
I will bring	Yo aportaré	Aport-	Ar changes to "aré"
You will bring	Tú aportarás		Ar changes to "arás"

He/She/It will bring	Él aportará		Ar changes to "ará"
We will bring	Nosotros aportaremos		Ar changes to "aremos"
You will bring	Ustedes aportarán		Ar changes to "arán"
They will bring	Ellos/Ellas aportarán		Ar changes to "arán"

The good thing is a job interview comes down to talking mostly about yourself. Therefore, it is important for you to know all the conjugations because you may want to talk about your plans for specific people or other departments. The main goal, however, is learning to talk about yourself.

Yo ah-por-tah-réh

Now, let's go through examples.

I will bring all my experience.	Yo aportaré toda mi experiencia.
He will bring many resources.	Él aportará muchos recursos.
We will bring a new selling strategy.	Nosotros aportaremos una nueva estrategia de ventas.
They will bring all the volunteers for this project.	Ellos aportarán todos los voluntarios para este proyecto.

It is time to go through our second termination: verbs that end in "-er".

Remember, you have to spot the root and then make the corresponding changes for every termination and conjugation. For the verb "aprender", the root is "aprend-".

To learn	Aprender	Root	Termination

I will learn	Yo aprenderé		Er changes to "eré"
You will learn	Tú aprenderás		Er changes to "erás"
He/She/It will learn	Él/Ella/Eso aprenderá	Aprend-	Er changes to "erá"
We will learn	Nosotros aprenderemos		Er changes to "eremos"
You will learn	Ustedes aprenderán		Er changes to "erán"
They will learn	Ellos/Ellas aprenderán		Er changes to "erán"

Again, let's take a moment to focus on you: ah-pren-deh-ré.

I will learn in this company.	Yo aprenderé dentro de esta compañía.

He will learn from this experience.	Él aprenderá con esta experiencia.
We will learn through hard work.	Nosotros aprenderemos a través del trabajo arduo.
They will learn a lot.	Ellos aprenderán mucho.

From a hiring perspective, "to lead" is a very important verb. Being able to lead is a well-appreciated skill for most recruiters, especially for some positions.

The root for the verb "dirigir" is "dirig-".

To lead	Dirigir	Root	Termination
I will lead	Yo dirigiré	Dirig-	Ir changes to "iré"
You will lead	Tú dirigirás		Ir changes to "irás"

He/She/It will lead	Él dirigirá		Ir changes to "irá"
We will lead	Nosotros dirigiremos		Ir changes to "iremos"
You will lead	Ustedes dirigirán		Ir changes to "irán"
They will lead	Ellos/Ellas dirigirán		Ir changes to "irán"

Yo-dee-ree-hee-reh

You will lead this project.	Tú dirigirás este proyecto.
She will lead this department.	Ella dirigirá este departamento.
We will lead the first part of the conference.	Nosotros dirigiremos la primera parte de la conferencia.

| They will lead us to success. | Ellos nos dirigirán al éxito. |

The next verb to look at is the verb "to be". It is with this verb that I first knew about the auxiliary for future (will) and its uses. More than that, it gives you a basic structure for putting sentences together in "futuro simple", the most commonly used tense for the future.

To be	**Ser**	**Estar**
I will be	Yo seré	Yo estaré
You will be	Tú serás	Tú estarás
He/She/It will be	Él será	Él estará
We will be	Nosotros seremos	Nosotros estaremos
You/They will be	Ustedes/Ellos/Ellas serán	Ustedes/Ellos/Ellas estarán

www.LearnLikeNatives.com

First, let's practice with the future tense of "ser".

I will be the leader in this project.	Yo seré el líder de este proyecto.
He will be a great asset to this team.	Él será un gran activo para este equipo.
This software will be great for us.	Este programa será genial para nosotros.
They will take care of everything.	Ellos se encargarán de todo.

Now, a few examples with the future tense of "estar".

I will be in a lead position this time.	Yo estaré en una posición de liderazgo esta vez.
He will be waiting for your instructions.	Él estará esperando por tus instrucciones.
This job will be waiting for you.	Este trabajo estará esperando por ti.

We will be in a meeting for the next hour.	Nosotros estaremos en una reunión por la próxima hora.

You can see that for Spanish, the words "will be" compress to form a simple idea: "seré o estaré". This is the Spanish form for "to be" that will happen in the future.

With this, you can create sentences talking about what you have planned for the future.

"With these changes, we will be the first company in our field."

"Con estos cambios, nosotros seremos la primera compañía en nuestro campo."

Now, let's check our final verb, "tener".

To have	**Tener**
I will have	Yo tendré
You will have	Tú tendrás

He/She/It will have	Él tendrá
We will have	Nosotros tendremos
You will have	Ustedes tendrán
They will have	Ellos/Ellas tendrán

"To have" is a great verb because it helps us build new tenses, as you have seen. In this case, we can use it in two ways: first, as the "future simple" form for having. Alternatively, you can use it to create the "future perfect", or "futuro perfecto", a tense that helps you indicate something that will happen somewhere between now and another point in the future. I should show you an example.

"I will have it ready by 2 pm."

"Lo tendré listo para las 2 pm."

This is a sentence using "futuro simple".

Pronoun + verb future.

"I will have done this by 2 pm."

"Lo habré terminado para las 2 pm."

This is a sentence written in "futuro perfecto".

Pronoun + "to have" in future + past participle.

This mix of future and past tense verbs create the complexity of the "future perfect".

I will have everything done by tonight.	Yo tendré todo listo para esta noche.
You will have been here for 2 years in one week.	Tú habrás estado aquí por dos años en una semana.
She will have made it if she passes this.	Ella lo habrá logrado si aprueba esto.
They will have done it by the weekend.	Ellos habrán hecho esto para el fin.

Yes. I can almost hear you talking. No worries. We will see more of these examples in the next dialogue.

Mr. King (Sr. King): Hello. Are you Leo Mitchell?

Hola. ¿Tú eres Leo Mitchell?

Leo: Good afternoon. Yes, I am.

Buenas tardes. Sí, lo soy.

Mr. King (Sr. King): Perfect. Please, come with me.

Perfecto. Por favor, ven conmigo.

Leo: Sure.

Seguro.

Mr. King (Sr. King): Tell me, Leo. If we hire you, what will you bring to the company?

Dime, Leo. Si te contratamos, ¿qué aportarás a la compañía?

Leo: I will bring 10-year experience in conflict and risk management.

Aportaré 10 años de experiencia en manejo de riesgos y conflicto.

Mr. King (Sr. King): *According to your knowledge, when will the updates be made?*

De acuerdo a tu conocimiento, ¿cuándo estarán hechas las actualizaciones?

Leo: *I will have updates done within the first semester of 2020.*

Tendré las actualizaciones listas durante el primer semestre de 2020.

Mr. King (Sr. King): *What will you need to achieve that?*

¿Qué necesitarás para conseguir eso?

Leo: *I will need a team, including two technicians.*

Necesitaré un equipo, incluidos dos técnicos.

Mr. King (Sr. King): *Very well. When will you start?*

Muy bien. ¿Cuándo comenzarás?

Leo: *Next week will be okay.*

La semana que viene estará bien.

I hope you are cracking this. All languages are about structure and, even if some are more complex than others, they become natural with time and practice. By the way, have you had a look at your new office?

Chapter 11 – New Job, New Life

I always get nervous on my first day working at a new place. But I think it is also exciting to meet new people, form new alliances, and basically have the chance to network in unknown circles.

Nervous or not, we are here to prepare you for what is coming. Do you want to join me?

Please, follow me into your new job.

Office	Oficina
This is your **office.**	Esta es tu **oficina.**

Oh-fee-si-nah

Computer	Computador
Your **computer** is ready to use.	Tu **computador** está listo para usar.

Kom-poo-tah-dor

Database	Base de datos
I granted you access to this **database.**	Te di acceso a esta **base de datos.**

Bah-se-the-da-tos

Yes! You are right! All of these expressions are similar to the ones you use! It will be a piece of cake!

Software	Programa
We have the best **software** to manage our database.	Tenemos el mejor **programa** para manejar nuestra base de datos.

Pro-gra-ma

Keyboard	Teclado
This is a nice **keyboard.**	Este es un buen **teclado.**

Teh-kla-doh

Monitor	Monitor
I need a larger **monitor.**	Necesito un **monitor** más grande.

Mo-ni-tor

The only difference between this word in English and in Spanish is where you put the accents in. While the stronger syllable in English is "mo", in Spanish it is in "tor". Remember to use a clear "t" to pronounce this.

Mouse	Ratón
My **mouse** is ergonomic.	Mi **ratón** es ergonómico.

Ra-tón

Hard drive	Disco duro
That is a 2 terabyte **hard drive.**	Ese es un **disco duro** de 2 terabyte.

This-coh-duh-roh

www.LearnLikeNatives.com

File	Archivo
You will find all that you need in the **file.**	Encontrarás todo lo que necesitas en el **archivo.**

R-chi-vo

Document	Documento
I already sent that **document.**	Ya envié ese **documento.**

Do-cu-men-to

Report	Informe
I will send the **report** this afternoon.	Enviaré el **informe** esta tarde.

In-for-meh

Coordinate	Coordinar

| We need to **coordinate** that meeting. | Necesitamos **coordinar** esa reunión. |

Kor-di-nar

| Desk | Escritorio |
| This is a nice **desk.** | Este es un buen **escritorio.** |

S-kri-toh-rio

| Department | Departamento |
| I work for the Human Resources **department.** | Yo trabajo para el **departamento** de Recursos Humanos. |

The-par-ta-men-to

| Coworker | Compañero de trabajo |
| I had lunch with a **coworker.** | Almorcé con un **compañero de trabajo.** |

Kom-pa-nie-ro the tra-bah-joh

See how many of these words are almost the same as English words, just with some small shifts?

Are you eager to practice? Great! Let's do this!

Eli: *How do you like your new office?*

¿Qué te parece tu nueva oficina?

Jace: *I like it a lot. I think I will need another monitor to split screens.*

Me gusta mucho. Creo que necesitaré otro monitor para dividir pantallas.

Eli: *Most coworkers do. We can coordinate that with the IT Department.*

La mayoría de los compañeros de trabajo lo hace. Podemos coordinarlo con el Departamento de tecnología.

Jace: *Perfect. Thank you. I love my desk.*

Perfecto. Gracias. Me encanta my escritorio.

Eli: *Yes. We invest in computers, software, and great equipment.*

Sí. Invertimos en computadores, programas y grandes equipos.

Jace: *When are you expecting to have the files you requested?*

¿Cuándo esperas tener los archivos que pediste?

Eli: *Tomorrow is fine.*

Mañana está bien.

Jace: *Good. I just have to add a few documents.*

Bien. Sólo tengo que agregar un par de documentos.

Eli: *Great, Jace! I think you will be a great addition to our team.*

¡Genial, Jace! Creo que serás una gran adición a nuestro equipo.

www.LearnLikeNatives.com

Jace: *Thank you for trusting in me. I will not let you down*

Gracias por confiar en mí. No te defraudaré.

How did you like your first day at the new office? Already familiar with the coffee machine? You should better get to work because now you have some big projects coming.

www.LearnLikeNatives.com

A Quick Message

A quick message before we start the final chapter of this book.

"No one can whistle a symphony. It takes a whole orchestra to play it." –

H.E. Luccock

Do you want to be part of the orchestra of the Learning Spanish community?

Here is how:

If you're enjoying this book, I would like to kindly ask you to leave a brief review on Amazon.

Reviews aren't easy to come by, but they have a profound impact in supporting my work. This way, I can keep creating new content to help the whole community at my very best.

I would be incredibly thankful if you could just take a minute to leave a quick review on Amazon, even if it's just a sentence or two!

www.LearnLikeNatives.com

It's that simple!

Thank you so much for taking the time to leave a short review on Amazon.

The community and I are very appreciative, as your review makes a difference.

Now, let's get back to learning Spanish

Chapter 12 – Bringing Home the Bacon

You have been preparing for this moment. You got yourself a new job, you have a new office and work team, and now is the time to start closing some business and bringing home the money. As always, let's first go with the essentials.

Meeting	Reunión
We have everything ready for the **meeting.**	Tenemos todo listo para la **reunión.**

Re-u-nion

Sell	Vender
We plan to **sell** when it reaches $95.	Nosotros planeamos **vender** cuando alcance $95.

Ven-der

Take your time to practice that final "r" sound.

Capital	Capital
We need to raise **capital**.	Necesitamos recaudar **capital**.

Ka-pi-tal

Market	Mercado
The **market** is shifting.	El **mercado** está cambiando.

Mer-ka-doh

How are your open vowels looking? "Ah" is a good sound to practice.

Stock market	Bolsa de valores
The **stock market** could crash.	La **bolsa de valores** podría colapsar.

Bol-sa the va-lo-res

Project	Proyecto
The new **project** is very complex.	El nuevo **proyecto** es bastante complejo.

Pro-jec-toh

Budget	Presupuesto
The available **budget** is 750k.	El **presupuesto** disponible es de 750k.

Pre-su-pooes-to

Presentation	Presentación
I'll have the **presentation** ready by 1 pm.	Tendré la **presentación** lista a la 1 pm.

Pre-sen-ta-sion

Supply	Oferta

The **supply** is decreasing for some commodities.	La **oferta** está disminuyendo para algunos productos básicos.

Offer-ta

Demand	Demanda
The people **demand** new solutions.	La gente **demanda** nuevas soluciones.

De-man-da

Experience	Experiencia
I have 7 years of professional **experience**.	Tengo 7 años de **experiencia** profesional.

Ex-pe-riehn-sia

Invoice	Factura
I will send you my **invoice**.	Te enviaré mi **factura**.

Fact-oo-ra

Credit	Crédito
They have great **credit.**	Ellos tienen un gran **crédito.**

Cré-di-to

Just like the English word, but you add a final "o".

Loan	Préstamo
I will pay half of the **loan.**	Yo pagaré la mitad del **préstamo.**

Pres-tah-moh

Taxes	Impuestos
I have to calculate my **taxes.**	Tengo que calcular mis **impuestos.**

Im-pooes-tohs

Investment	Inversión
It is a great **investment**.	Es una gran **inversión**.

In-ver-sion

Spend	Gastar
It is important to **spend** in quality.	Es importante **gastar** en calidad.

Gas-tar

Save	Ahorrar
We can **save** up to 30%.	Podemos **ahorrar** hasta un 30%.

Ah-ho-rrar

Lose	Perder

www.LearnLikeNatives.com

| Sometimes you need to lose. | A veces necesitas **perder.** |

Per-der

Here we are. This is the final test. This chapter's practice is meant to gather general knowledge from the last three chapters. Are you ready to buckle? Don't be scared. You got this.

Mr. Reed (Sr. Reed): *I am going to be clear: I want a company to protect my investment.*

Yo voy a ser claro: quiero una compañía que proteja mi inversión.

Mr. Evans: *Perfect. I can offer you all my experience for that job.*

Perfecto. Puedo ofrecerte toda mi experiencia para ese trabajo.

Mr. Reed: *What will be your strategy?*

¿Cuál será tu estrategia?

Mr. Evans: *You have good credit. I plan to use a loan and increase the supply.*

Ustedes poseen buen crédito. Planeo usar un préstamo para aumentar la oferta.

Mr. Reed: *How will I save capital that way?*

¿Cómo ahorraré capital de esa manera?

Mr. Evans: *By covering for the demand, I expect a rise in the Stock Market.*

Al cubrir la demanda, espero un alza en la Bolsa de Valores.

Mr. Reed: *That will not do it alone.*

Solo eso no lo logrará.

Mr. Evans: *I know. That is why we have a strategy to increase our market share by 3%.*

Lo sé. Por eso tenemos una estrategia para incrementar su cuota de mercado en un 3%.

Mr. Reed: *Very well. I expect that you will have a great presentation for my board meeting.*

Muy bien. Espero que tengas una gran presentación para mi reunión de junta.

Mr. Evans: *You know I will. My budget projections do not lie.*

Tú sabes que sí. Mis proyecciones de presupuesto no mienten.

Mr. Reed: *All right. I expect your invoice, then.*

Muy bien. Espero tu factura, entonces.

Mr. Evans: *I will be sending it tomorrow.*

La estaré enviando mañana.

I want to know your opinion. How was this practice for you? Ask yourself, how can you improve? As I have been saying from the beginning, it is up to you to master these phrases and words. And practice is the only way to do it--talking and listening, repeatedly.

Conclusion

Congratulations on making it through to the end of this book! You now have all the tools you need to achieve your Spanish goals.

This is no science. Of course, there is a method, but it is mostly practicing, repeating, and doing! So, go for it. If you find yourself feeling unsure about something, just come back and look it up, and we'll go through it together! Yet, I am sure you already know so much, even more than you realize!

Look at all the things we did: we learned how to plan a trip, we discussed how to act if you or your family get sick, reviewed how to move around the city, ask for directions, and we had a nice conversation about how to talk about the past and the future.

We also learned how to deal with business in Spanish: we talked about how to present a CV and become an employee. Also, we went through some commercial and business Spanish to help you make great deals if you find yourself covering a management position.

Do you realize all the new things you can communicate now? You now have more resources for survival and regular living in a completely new environment, and I want to give you a big pat on the back for coming this far.

You can find the rest of the books in the series, as well as a whole host of other resources, at **LearnLikeNatives.com**. Simply add the book to your library to take the next step in your language learning journey. If you are ever in need of new ideas or direction, refer to our 'Speak Like a Native' eBook, available to you for free at **LearnLikeNatives.com**, which clearly outlines practical steps you can take to continue learning any language you choose.

Nevertheless, did I mention we are not over yet?

Now the fun part begins: try to watch in Spanish your favorite cartoons, or try with some famous TV series, of course with Spanish subtitles (yes Spanish subtitles, you can make it!). I would advise you, *Ugly Betty* (in Spanish, it is called *Betty la Fea)*. It's a big classic, easy, and fun to follow, yet extremely helpful for improving your Spanish!

Again, thank you for reading. I hope to meet you in the near future so we can learn even more!

www.LearnLikeNatives.com

www.LearnLikeNatives.com

Learn Like a Native is a revolutionary **language education brand** that is taking the linguistic world by storm. Forget boring grammar books that never get you anywhere, Learn Like a Native teaches you languages in a fast and fun way that actually works!

As an international, multichannel, language learning platform, we provide **books, audio guides and eBooks** so that you can acquire the knowledge you need, swiftly and easily.

Our **subject-based learning**, structured around real-world scenarios, builds your conversational muscle and ensures you learn the content most relevant to your requirements.
Discover our tools at *LearnLikeNatives.com*

When it comes to learning languages, we've got you covered!

www.ingramcontent.com/pod-product-compliance
Lightning Source LLC
Chambersburg PA
CBHW071726080526
44588CB00013B/1916